Mindful Learning

Mindful Learning

Teaching Self-Discipline and Academic Achievement

David B. Strahan

CAROLINA ACADEMIC PRESS

Durham, North Carolina

Library of Congress Cataloging-in-Publication Data

Strahan, David B.
   Mindful learning : teaching self-discipline and academic achievement
/ David B. Strahan.
       p.   cm.
   Includes bibliographical references (p.   ).
   ISBN 0-89089-932-0
   1. Affective education—United States.   2. Experiential learning—
United States.   3. Academic achievement—United States.   4. Self-
control—Study and teaching—United States.   5. Learning, Psychol-
ogy of.   I. Title.
LB1072.S87   1997
370.15'23—dc21   97-37448
                                                              CIP

CAROLINA ACADEMIC PRESS
700 Kent Street
Durham, North Carolina 27701
Telephone (919) 489-7486
Fax (919) 493-5668
www.cap-press.com

Printed in the United States of America

NOTE: David Strahan took the photographs in this text for illustration purposes only. Students and parents gave their consent to publish the photographs selected. The photographs serve to illustrate general ideas and do not offer identification of the hypothetical students mentioned in the text.

Dedication

This text is dedicated to John and Martha Strahan. Caring in action is the theme of this book because it has been the theme of their lives. They are the best teachers I have ever known. All three of their children became teachers. Two of us married teachers. All that "school talk" at the dinner table was the beginning of Mindful Learning. I hope I have captured the spirit of the conversation.

Contents

Foreword

Teaching for understanding has long been the hallmark of successful instruction. As a youngster, I often heard my grandmother describe her early years in teaching. She began her career in 1920. She liked to tell us about the strategies she used to connect learning experiences in her classroom with her students' day-to-day lives in a rural community. As a graduate of Miami University, she learned to teach using the "project approach" which emphasized "learning by doing." To her, it seemed a natural way to teach. Until her retirement in 1962, she taught with projects. Some of my happiest summer memories are of the days I spent with her, "practicing" projects she might use with her fifth graders the next fall.

In recent years, I have realized how much of my inspiration for teaching comes from my grandmother. I have begun to see how she inspired my father to teach, and my sisters, and how good teaching becomes part of the fabric of who we are.

I often wonder what my grandmother would think of teaching today. If she were still alive, I imagine she could enter just about any fifth grade classroom and quickly engage students in learning. I am not sure how she would react to the "skill and drill" approach she would find in some schools however. To her, it made more sense to emphasize learning by doing. It fit what she knew about teaching ten- and eleven-year-olds.

That same insight drives successful teachers in today's schools. Like my grandmother, they draw from a wisdom of practice. Unlike my grandmother, they can also draw from a growing body of research regarding learning and teaching. That research undergirds the 1995 publication of *This we believe* by the National Middle School Association. The authors of that document call for teachers to meet the needs of students through "curriculum that is challenging, integrative, and exploratory." They insist that "curriculum is integrative when it helps students make sense out of their life experiences" (p. 22).

That phrase, "making sense out of their life experiences," describes the essence of this text. In my work with teachers and researchers, I have developed an approach to teaching that encourages students to connect the issues that concern them with their experiences in classrooms. These connections foster personal well-being as well as academic success. Students understand more about themselves as learners and assume more responsibility and self-discipline. We have called our approach Mindful Learning to emphasize the power of different frames of mind and the importance of thoughtfulness in lessons.

Mindful Learning has taken shape through the contributions of teachers and students over the past four years. Jamestown Middle School in Guilford County, North Carolina has been our living laboratory. I want to thank all of the teachers and student teachers who have brought *Mindful Learning* to life. I especially want to thank the sixth, seventh, and eighth graders who gave our lessons so much energy. Some of them are pictured throughout the text.

Three members of our *Mindful Learning* team merit more appreciation than I can express in these pages. For the first two years, Heidi Summey provided constant support in nurturing *Mindful Learning* at JMS. More recently, Sally Smith has served as editorial advisor and reader extraordinaire. When it came time for production, Linda Lacy, my editor at Carolina Academic Press, came to my rescue with everything I needed to know about book writing and with patient corrections. All three of them deserve a great deal of thanks for helping shape this text.

I think my grandmother would find much familiar in *Mindful Learning*. I think she would be pleased that research on teaching has embellished her wisdom of practice, that we know more about working with individual students, and that we are learning to make lessons more inclusive. I think she would be especially pleased to know that research has confirmed what she believed so strongly in her heart, that good teaching begins with relationships, that no matter how sophisticated our technology becomes, the teacher, as a person, remains the instrument of instruction.

Mindful Learning

CHAPTER-TO-CHAPTER CONNECTIONS

This first chapter presents an overview of Mindful Learning. Mindful Learning offers a systematic approach to promoting caring in action in the classroom. The Mindful Learning framework reflects what we know about how the "mind" works best and how successful teachers promote "learning." In describing the Mindful Learning approach, this chapter highlights the following connections:

- Successful teachers integrate efforts to care for students as people, the "affective" portion of the curriculum, with efforts to enrich their understanding of content, the "academic" dimension of instruction.
- Successful teachers accomplish this integration by providing both structure and support.
- Successful teachers encourage students to develop self-worth and self-discipline by helping them understand what matters to them and learn to perform in those areas.
- Successful schools promote caring by responding to students as individuals, helping them learn to care for other people, and building on their interests.

This description of Mindful Learning provides a foundation for the rest of the book. The chapter that follows shows how Mindful Learning integrates theories about learning with research on successful teaching. The three chapters in the second section illustrate specific strategies that promote success. The concluding portion of the book offers suggestions for creating caring communities for learning through improved teamwork.

Chapter One

Mindful Learning: Integrating emotional and academic development

The best thing about my school is the teachers and my friends. Our teachers are real neat and they like us a lot, well most of them do. I would not want to go to another school because it would be hard to get to know new people. Here I know where everything is and I know the teachers' names, and which ones are nice, and which ones are mean. Sixth grade was fun because I learned a lot and got to see my friends.
—Jackie, 11, 7th grade

I think I am handling myself better than I did in the past. I haven't been in as many fights. This school is really boring though. None of my friends are here any more. I am tired of everyone looking at me. I would like them to know that I am not a bad kid or crazy or a lunatic even though I have a bad temper and sometimes say things I don't mean.
—Daniel, 15, 7th grade

Jackie and Daniel have experienced school very differently. Jackie feels a sense of belonging. She has grown closer to her classmates and teachers. She has learned new concepts and gained confidence in herself. Daniel has grown weary of school. As soon as he is old enough, he might drop out. His decision may depend on how his teachers respond to his needs. Fortunately, there are ways to make school more inviting for Daniel while continuing to encourage Jackie.

As a teacher educator, I have spent more than one thousand days in schools over the past twenty years: talking with students, studying successful teachers, joining them in teaching lessons, reflecting with college students learning to teach, and meeting with teams to support school improvement. I have learned a great deal about how teachers can encourage students like Jackie to succeed and ways that they can reach students like Daniel more effectively.

5

Successful teachers thrive on this challenge of meeting students' needs. Many of the talented teachers I met twenty years ago are teaching with even more energy these days: finding ways to connect with students, developing creative lessons, providing leadership with their colleagues. Others have grown frustrated and left the profession. Some teachers have returned to college to get advanced degrees in education. Others have asked about graduate programs that might help them "escape" from teaching.

Recent studies have shown that one of the biggest differences between surviving and thriving in teaching is the ability to balance the conflicting demands of the profession (Sternberg and Horvath, 1995). On one hand, teachers try to teach "the whole child," to nurture emotional development, and help students become better people. On the other hand, teachers need to be accountable, to increase test scores and "cover" the curriculum. Somehow, successful teachers have learned to do both. They integrate efforts to care for students as people, the "affective" portion of the curriculum, with efforts to enrich their understanding of content, the "academic" dimension of instruction. Our best evidence suggests that teaching for understanding always involves caring for students as individuals (Strahan, 1995). We have learned that there are two connected issues to successful schooling:

1) how well adults structure educational experiences for students

2) how well adults support students and each other.

This essential combination of structure and support is "caring in action."

"Caring in action" is the theme of this book. The chapters that follow describe how successful teachers connect caring for their students with decisions about their lessons. Each chapter presents specific elements of "Mindful Learning." Over the past four years, I have worked with teachers to integrate what we have learned about caring and action. We have incorporated what we know about how the "mind" works best with what we know about how to promote "learning." The resulting framework for Mindful Learning has proven successful in promoting caring in action (Strahan, Summey, and Bowles, 1996).

Each of the chapters in the book examines one of the basic ele-

Figure 1.1 An Overview of Mindful Learning

CONNECTING CARING AND ACTION
- Integrating emotional and academic development
- Connecting theory, research, and practice

MINDFUL LEARNING

TEACHING FOR SUCCESS
- Promoting academic achievement
- Encouraging self-discipline
- Assessing progress toward success

TEAMING FOR SCHOOL IMPROVEMENT
- Creating caring communities for learning
- Promoting teamwork among teachers
- Helping students learn teamwork

ments of Mindful Learning. The two chapters in the first section explore specific ways teachers connect caring and action. The three chapters in the second section illustrate strategies that promote success. The concluding portion of the book offers suggestions for creating caring communities for learning through improved teamwork. Figure 1.1 presents an overview of the text.

Mindful Learning and teaching

The following vignette portrays some of the ways that teachers have applied the concept of Mindful Learning. For illustration purposes, I have projected Jackie and Daniel into this classroom composite. In this composite, the teacher, Ms. Johnson, makes instructional decisions based on what she knows about her students and what she observes as they process information.

The students in Ms. Johnson's seventh-grade class have been studying human growth and development. They began by reading a passage in their science book (Figure 1.2) that described the stages of human development. As they discussed some of the general patterns described, students began to raise questions about

Figure 1.2 — Adolescence

Adolescence is a time when growth and development once again become very rapid. During this period of life, hormone production plays a most important role. Specific hormones interact with each other in many ways. For example, hormones trigger a rapid increase in bone and muscle size. This increase is not a smooth or gradual one. Sometimes it seems that almost overnight arms and legs become longer. Hands and feet often grow to an adult size before the rest of the body.

The rapid growth spurt in size of muscles and bones may cause clumsiness. Teenagers should remember that this is normal and temporary. An adolescent's appearance also changes as body parts grow and develop. These changes do not occur with all body parts at the same time. This often causes adolescents to be sensitive about their appearance. But with time, growth evens out, producing the well-proportioned face and body of an adult.

At this same time, development of the reproduction system is occurring. Puberty begins when the pituitary gland located in the skull stimulates the secretion of the sex hormones. These sex hormones trigger the development of the reproductive system and the secondary sex characteristics (such as beard growth in males) that we associate with adulthood. Also during puberty, other hormones, such as those that cause growth, become active.

Puberty actually lasts for several years. The rate of development greatly varies from individual to individual. Sweat glands and skin secretions change during puberty. This may result in skin problems and new body odors. For this reason, the adolescent needs to be increasingly aware of physical hygiene.

The increased production of hormones also affects the moods of the adolescent. Mood swings are common in puberty. Friendships that once were open and easy may become difficult as teenagers experience and deal with their own feelings and those of their friends. Adolescence is a time when the body and mind ready themselves for adulthood. It is a time of value development and identity formation. Increasing responsibility and freedom can make the time of adolescence both exciting and challenging.

Source: Hill, S.R., Shaw, R., Stiffler, L.E., Lacy, L. (1994) *Integrated Science: Systems and Diversity* Durham, North Carolina: Carolina Academic Press.

their own development. They noted that while the text offered general information about adolescence, it contained very little information regarding early adolescence.

When Michael asked, "Where do we fit into this? Are we in 'middle childhood' or 'adolescence?'" questions began to fly. Susan wanted to know why the text did not mention seventh grade. Jackie asked if questions about puberty would be answered in health class. John wondered if anyone had studied what kids think about these changes. When Ms. Johnson asked the students how they might begin to explore their questions systematically, Jackie suggested that they write down their questions.

Ms. Johnson asked students to meet in task groups to begin listing questions. After several animated discussions across two days, the class had compiled two different lists of questions. Their list of "shared questions" was a summary of things they thought everyone in the class wanted to know. "Unique questions" were those posed by individual students or task groups. Study plans for investigating their shared questions were mapped out on large paper on one of the bulletin boards (see Shared Questions/Study Plans chart).

On Wednesday of the second week, Ms. Johnson circulated from group to group, helping students with final preparations for their reports. Jackie, Keith, Ron, and Kelly reviewed the note cards they had made from their reading in the library on physical growth during puberty. Ms. Johnson helped them decide which items they wanted to share in their oral report and which facts they wanted their classmates to read about in the booklets they had prepared for

SHARED QUESTIONS	STUDY PLANS
1. How do our bodies change during puberty?	• Gather library resources. • Summarize the most impor tant concepts on notecards. • Prepare oral reports for general information. • Write mini-reports on more personal aspects of puberty.
2. How do we feel about these changes?	• Draft questions for peer survey. • Decide which questions to use. • Give survey to all seventh graders. • Analyze and illustrate results.
3. What do older students think about the changes they experienced?	• Prepare interview questions for high school students. • Tape-record interviews and take pictures.
4. How does the media portray our experiences and what do students other countries think?	• Videotape TV shows that youth culture. • Select songs and images. • Create artwork to help illustrate responses. • Check internet for additional information.

independent reading. They had confided in Ms. Johnson that they thought some of the facts would be "embarrassing" to talk about in an oral report. She suggested that they write mini-reports as booklets for students to read privately. Today she helped them make final plans for sharing the booklets with a parent committee for approval.

Tamika, Jack, Susan, and Chad worked at the art center. They were illustrating charts and graphs which reported the results from their survey of how the seventh graders in their school felt about growing up. They had written seventeen questions for their survey and the rest of the class had helped them select the eight best questions. They were now drawing their graphs for each question onto poster boards and looking for pictures from magazines to illustrate responses.

Aaron, Melissa, Martin, and Jill worked at a computer station.

Ms. Johnson reviewed the procedures they would need to follow to mix the pictures they had taken with the sound bites they had recorded at the high school. They had interviewed students about their memories of middle school and their feelings about the changes they had experienced during those years.

Erica, Maria, Daniel, and Juan were working with the VCR, preparing their presentation about cultural perspectives on early adolescence. They reviewed the videotaped clips they had recorded from a music special entitled "Rock around the World." They were deciding which of the video clips would provide the best conclusion to their presentation.

Kristin and Jerome edited a draft of their report on how they thought American teenagers had responded to the video. Warren and Kendra returned from the art room to report on their progress with the sculptures they were doing on the four different views of growing up mentioned in the songs. Before class ended, Ms. Johnson asked each group for a brief progress report and reminded the class to invite their friends and family to attend the "world premier" of their show Thursday night.

This brief vignette demonstrates Mindful Learning in action. While Ms. Johnson is a composite of teachers I know, this classroom vignette represents my definition of Mindful Learning. Ms. Johnson has designed activities that fit what she knows about her seventh graders. She knows they learn best when they begin with questions that matter to them, when they have opportunities to explore these questions in their own ways, and when they can create connections among ideas, She appreciates their need to socialize and builds in time for "academic" talk. She also understands that some of them like to work alone at times. She helps them express their ideas in ways that reflect their varying ways of learning. She sees her role as both guide and encourager. As a result, she creates connections WITH her students rather than teaching TO them.

Ms. Johnson has blended academic instruction with the affective curriculum in a natural fashion. Her students are learning essential concepts of the science curriculum. They are also learning to work in teams, to accept responsibility, and to make choices. Ms. Johnson's classroom may seem futuristic. While few classrooms are equipped with all of the technology mentioned, most of the technology is available in some form in most middle schools.

The most important aspect of Ms. Johnson's Mindful Learning approach is that ALL of the students in her class are involved in learning. Daniel, who may feel alienated at other times of the day, knows that Ms. Johnson will offer him opportunities to use his talents to contribute to the lesson. In this vignette, he can incorporate his interests in music and art into his group project on "cultural perspectives on early adolescence." Ms Johnson and her teammates understand that Daniel has grown school weary. Rather than single him out for special classes or individualized interventions, they are trying to help him understand how he learns best and what he might draw from school. Jackie, who seems to enjoys school most of the time, is even more involved in these lessons because she has the same opportunities to choose and contribute.

This vignette emphasizes what is possible rather than what exists at the moment. Even so, teachers can begin to implement a Mindful Learning approach immediately. What is most important is a clear understanding of the basic notion of student-centered teaching and a commitment to begin to work toward more exploratory instruction.

A Rationale for Mindful Learning

In recent years, we have become more aware of developmental transitions. Teachers and parents talk about ways to build self-concept, enhance self-esteem, and encourage self-confidence. Community groups and governmental agencies have focused more attention on the needs of youth. Even so, the connections between self-concept and achievement have often been misinterpreted. In our efforts to support children in transition, we have sometimes confused the need for them to "feel good' about themselves with the need to learn self-discipline. Some programs, while well intended, have disconnected feeling good from accomplishment. Research now shows that, more than anything else, middle- level students need to develop views of themselves as valuable, able, and responsible people (Purkey and Novak, 1995).

Developing self-worth

One of the most useful studies of these developmental needs is Harter's (1990) analysis of the evolution of self-worth across the lifespan. Harter proposes a model of self-worth that integrates "competence" and "social support." Her studies indicate that individuals with the highest self-worth are those who see themselves doing well in areas they feel are important and who see themselves as having a high degree of social support (p. 80).

Her studies describe how these perceptions grow developmentally. She offers evidence that young children depend on the perceptions of "significant others" in forming their notions of competence. As children enter middle childhood, they are able to express at least five domains of self-concept: scholastic competence, athletic competence, physical appearance, peer acceptance, and behavioral conduct (p. 71). Harter suggests that students' views of themselves are shaped by their perceptions regarding "competence." Their self perceptions stem from their own judgements of how well they think they perform tasks that matter to them and how they view the judgements of other people who matter to them.

The development of self-worth occurs in an interactive fashion. Observations of youth sports often illustrate these dynamics. When young children play soccer, for example, there are usually one or two players who do not seem to get into the game. This is especially the case with four- and five-year-olds. With this age group, players sometimes leave the field during the game, pose for pictures on the sideline, or stop chasing the ball to talk to a friend. In one of our son's games, his team scored a goal when the goalie and both fullbacks on the other team left the field to play a game of tag behind the net. Even so, when the players came off the field and the parents and coaches congratulated them for playing, everyone was happy. Harter's studies suggest that young children internalize what the coaches, parents, or significant others tell them. If children are told "good game," indications are that they tend to believe that message.

That is no longer the case for young adolescents. By the time they approach puberty, children form very clear views of themselves as "athletes." If a player completes a game without ever kicking the ball and the coach congratulates that player for "good play," Harter's studies suggest that the player is not likely to believe the coach. In the years since early childhood, the player has developed a fairly specific concept of "good play"–a mental picture that develops from observing other players, comparing performances, and internalizing verbal and nonverbal messages. This construct of "good play" becomes very specific. Young adolescent players can tell us a great deal about the characteristics of "good players," who they are, what they do well, and why these skills are important. Moreover, they can tell us how they think they fit into a rank ordering of good players, listing who they think is better and why.

The same is true for "good math students," "good readers," and "good friends." Young adolescents believe they are "competent" in an area of performance when they receive social support from significant others AND their performance approximates their concept of "good performance."

Many of us would argue that the development of self-worth is the most important aspect of growing up. This learning process is much more than young people "feeling good" about who they are. How they feel about themselves is determined by what matters to them and how they perform in those areas. This means that as parents, teachers, and administrators, we must remember that self-worth is learned and that we play an important part in that learning. Achievement, self-concept, and motivation are inseparable. To help bolster our students' feelings of self-worth, we must help them learn ways they can control their thoughts and feelings.

Developing self-discipline

In our discussions with parents and teachers, we also hear a great deal about self-discipline. Parents sometimes wish their children could control themselves better. Teachers wish they did not have to focus so much on discipline. Communities wonder why so many youth seem "out of control."

Like self-worth, self-discipline is learned. Learning self-discipline requires the development of processes of self-control. Those young defenders who left the soccer field to play tag probably thought very little about their decision. Older players would think differently about leaving the field. They would be more likely to monitor their decisions based on constructs of right/wrong or good play/poor play. These constructs would have evolved from observations of other players, experience in games, and comments from their coaches. They would have internalized all of this information and established "control" over their game decisions. One of the most powerful frameworks for helping us understand how children develop internal regulation is Glasser's (1993) control theory.

Glasser began his research as a practicing psychiatrist. Realizing that patients needed to assume responsibility for their plans of action, he developed the *Reality Therapy* approach to counseling (Glasser, 1965). He began using this approach with at-risk adolescents in juvenile treatment centers. He found that these same basic strategies were successful. He encouraged young people to think through their choices, consider the consequences and accept responsibility for their decisions. He began working with teachers in several schools to provide even broader applications. The result of this research was *Schools without Failure* (1969), an integrated framework for providing school experiences that facilitate the development of self-discipline. As his work continued, he developed increasingly sophisticated approaches to both counseling and schooling, first through *Control Theory* (1984) and *Control Theory in the Classroom* (1986) and most recently, in *The Quality School* (1990) and *The Quality School Teacher* (1993). In all of his work, Glasser has emphasized two essential principles:

1. We choose our behaviors and are responsible for the choices we make.
2. Our choices are attempts to attempts to meet five basic needs: security, belonging, power, freedom, and fun. (Glasser, 1993, 123–137).

Glasser (1986) argued that most of the behaviors that occur in school (and elsewhere) reflect the efforts of students, teachers, and administrators to "control" events to satisfy one or more of these basic needs. Students (and teachers) need to feel physically and psychologically secure, to feel that they belong, to feel empowered, to have opportunities to make choices, to feel challenged and to have fun. When these needs are not met, students "misbehave" by trying to establish control in inappropriate ways: avoiding class, seeking attention, creating diversions, or playing "power games."

The cognitive processes involved in attempting to establish control and meet these basic needs are often difficult to understand. Glasser described these processes as the creation and modification of "mental pictures."

> What control theory teaches is that everything we do is initiated by a satisfying picture of that activity that we store in our heads as a pleasant memory. (p. 34)

Students who see themselves as troublemakers are acting out their pictures of themselves. For example, a student who works the system to get suspended may have internalized a picture of himself "in control and having fun" when he is out with the guys in his neighborhood. When he feels threatened, rejected, neglected, or bored in school, his picture of himself in his neighborhood becomes a goal. Even though he may not be fully conscious of this goal, he makes choices that result in suspension. His picture may not be realistic. He may be suspended only to find his friends are in school and his neighborhood quiet but, unless his picture changes, his behavior pattern will repeat itself.

Glasser suggested that there are only two reasons why pictures change: significant others and successful experiences (p. 39). Teachers and administrators who have gained students' trust may help them develop new pictures. These new pictures are most powerful when they are the result of tangible success. Developing new pictures requires taking risks. Students (and teachers) cannot try out new notions of themselves unless they take chances: trusting someone, trying a new activity, risking some failure in the process. Control theory can help us understand this process.

Teaching self-worth and self-discipline

This brief analysis of ways that students learn self-worth and self-discipline provides a basis for understanding more about the teacher's role in nurturing both affective and academic development. One important conclusion is the importance of integrating efforts to teach content with efforts to teach "the whole child." Such integration requires a careful balancing of priorities.

Some educators believe young adolescents are "out-of-control." Based on that belief, they have created "controlling" institutions, schools where the primary agenda is order and obedience. Other educators, while perhaps not as numerous, believe that young adolescents need to feel good about everything. Based on that belief, they try to shelter students from any negative experiences. Successful educators balance these beliefs. They understand that young adolescents need both **structure** and **support**.

As indicated earlier in this chapter, Mindful Learning provides a systematic approach to teaching with structure and support. Based on a synthesis of control theory and research on teaching to diversity, Mindful Learning emphasizes thinking about how students learn and, in particular, how they learn self-discipline and how they learn to be successful in school. **The basic goal of Mindful**

Learning is to teach academic concepts and self-discipline in ways that tap students' strengths. Mindful Learning links theory with practice by beginning with strategies that help students understand how they learn best, incorporating these strategies into lessons and units, and extending these strategies to help students think through the decisions they make about their schoolwork and their behavior. Our action research studies have convinced us that Mindful Learning integrates support and structure in helping students address developmental issues (Strahan, Summey, & Bowles, 1996; Summey and Strahan, 1997). The rest of this book describes ways to put Mindful Learning into practice.

Beyond the Mindful classroom: A vision of successful schooling

Studies of successful middle-level schools document the importance of integrating support and structure. In *Successful Schools for Young Adolescents,* Lipsitz (1984) presents vivid case studies of four schools that meet the needs of their students in extraordinary ways. In her final chapter, as she considers what seems to matter most in accomplishing their success and how other schools might learn from them, she concludes that "to become a good middle-grade school requires a change in vision about the possibilities of educating young adolescents" (p. 200).

The term "vision" has certainly grown more prevalent since Lipsitz published her report. Administrators often speak of vision. Most schools have drafted a vision statement. Some schools have "vision teams" and "vision posters" hanging on their walls. Real vision, of course, is much deeper.

In a comprehensive analysis of the challenges of today's schools and the needs of today's youth, Noddings (1992) describes an "alternative vision" of schooling based on "caring." Her comprehensive review of recent efforts toward school improvement chronicles the ways that we have made "shallow responses to deep social changes" (p. 1). She characterizes many of our attempts to improve schooling through organizational changes and policy initiatives as technical innovations "designed to address isolated bits of the problem" (p. 1). She suggests that efforts to revise the curricu-

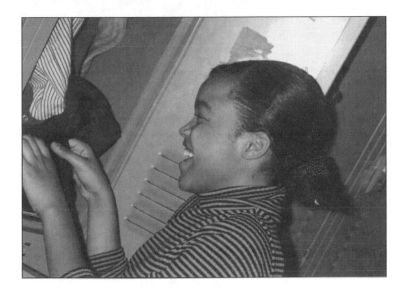

lum, improve classroom management, and enhance instruction have often been misdirected searches for simple solutions. She argues that we must begin to rethink our purposes and to focus on the human relations that constitute meaningful education.

Noddings insists that our main goal should be "to promote the growth of students as healthy, competent, moral people" (p. 10). To reach this goal, we must focus on caring as it occurs among students and teachers. Real caring, she insists, means responding "differentially" to students, helping them learn to care, and basing instruction on their experiences and interests (p. 19). She describes how we might reconfigure schools around "centers of caring:" caring for self, caring for family and friends, caring for others, caring for the earth, and caring for ideas (p. 47).

Sometimes the challenge to promote caring seems overwhelming. As adults, we are often tempted to believe that our opinions and actions may not matter, that students respond only to their peers. Fortunately, we have powerful evidence that adults can be very influential.

In a ten-year study of adolescents and their communities, Ianni (1989) found that students' values reflected the "shared understandings" of their communities (p. 680).

> For example, if we asked a teenager why he or she did or did not become involved in some activity, seek some goal, avoid

some risk, or behave in some way rather than another, the reason was seldom said to be because of any specific rule or authority system, such as family or peers. Rather, we heard much more generalized reasons such as, "I don't know why, but it seemed to be the right thing to do" or "That's the way it is here in Sheffield." (p. 680)

Ianni called this "unwritten, 'sensed' set of expectations and standards" a community's "youth charter" (p. 680). Ianni and his colleagues found that caring adults can play a critical role in defining and transmitting powerful notions about "the way we do things around here." Cultural impact was more often local than regional or national. In fact, this ten-year study found little evidence of a "national" youth culture and documented ways that adults in specific local settings had created "better social environments" that encouraged dramatic changes in the lives of young people (p. 679). Ianni and his colleagues concluded that the adults in a community can provide a supportive context in which positive "youth charters" are more likely to evolve.

Conclusions

Successful teachers have learned to integrate the teaching of content with the nurturing of self-discipline. They understand that today's youth face unique challenges in connecting choices and consequences. Students face the same developmental issues that young people have always encountered, yet they do so in times that offer little certainty. Harter's perspective on growing up, Glasser's theories of development, Noddings' framework for caring, and Ianni's study of community provide a powerful foundation for understanding today's students and responding to their needs. Caring for self, others, and ideas is the hallmark of a successful school. Educators can nurture caring by providing both structure and support. Mindful Learning is one approach that has proven effective in teaching self-worth and self-discipline. Mindful Learning grows even more powerful when it becomes a perspective that is shared across a school community committed to caring in action.

The rest of this text illustrates ways to put the theory of Mindful Learning into action. The text is organized to address the essential tasks of teaching: motivation, curriculum, planning, evaluation, management, and professional development. Chapter Two links theory to practice by detailing the planning processes involved in Mindful Learning. Chapter Three highlights specific strategies for promoting academic success with carefully designed instructional strategies. Chapter Four integrates all of these strategies in teaching self-discipline through comprehensive classroom management. Chapter Five offers specific suggestions for assessing progress. Chapter Six connects the themes of the text by suggesting ways that teachers, parents, administrators, and students can work together to create caring communities for learning.

Each chapter offers illustrations of classroom dynamics and integrates these illustrations with reviews of research on successful teaching. Each of the chapters features "classroom ready" materials that teachers can immediately put into practice. At the end of each chapter is an additional **"Classroom Application"** that presents lesson ideas in greater detail. Each chapter concludes with **"Research Abstracts"** that summarize recent data-based studies and provide sources for further reference and continued reading. In preparing these materials, I have tried to focus on the needs of students like Jackie and Daniel and the hope that their future teachers will help us extend our collective wisdom of practice.

Classroom Applications
"Exploring Youth Culture"

Purpose: These activities provide students an opportunity to analyze the ways that popular culture portrays youth. Students can compare their views of these cultural images with those of their classmates. Teachers can glimpse some of the ways students perceive themselves, collectively and individually. The activity can be integrated into almost any content emphasis (language arts, math, science, social studies, health, art, or music) or used as part of a "home base" advisory program.

Directions:

1. Gather examples of popular culture (video clips, music videos, newspaper/magazine articles, advertisements, posters, T-shirts, etc.)
2. Ask students to select one of the following investigations:

Age group surveys—Write five questions to ask people of different ages that relate to values. For example: What is most important to you about your career choice? your friends? your leisure time? Ask these questions to at least three different groups of people: retirees, people in their 30s and 40s, people in their late teens or early 20s.

Messages from merchandise—Analyze the logos and print messages on at least five different T-shirts. What are the messages? How do people respond?

Musical messages/song lyrics—Compare and contrast two different songs that portray ideas or feelings related to being an adolescent.

Peer interviews—Write five questions to ask classmates that relate to values such as: What is most important to you about your career choice? your friends? your leisure time? Ask these questions to at least six different people.

Reflective journal—Think back to what it was like to be in fourth grade, second grade, or preschool. Write about some of your most vivid memories. How have your ideas and feelings changed?

Visual images—Analyze the messages from at least five different advertisements aimed at young people. What are the messages? Do they portray youth positively or negatively? How do people respond?

3. Ask each group to prepare and present a brief report that addresses the following questions:

What images of youth did you identify?

Did these images include any stereotypes? If so, what were they?

What messages about growing up are suggested?

How would you modify these messages?

What have you learned about the ways that our culture portrays young people? about your own views of youth? about how you learn best?

RESEARCH ABSTRACTS

(summaries of two of the data-based studies referenced in this chapter as a resource for further reference and continued reading)

Harter, S. (1990). Causes, correlates, and the functional role of global self-worth: A life-span perspective. In R. Sternberg & J. Kolligan (Eds.), *Competence considered* **(pp. 67–97). New Haven, CT: Yale University Press.**

In a comprehensive analysis of the development of self-worth across the life span, Harter reviews a series of investigations conducted with children, adolescents, college students, and adults. Results provide a strong body of evidence that "global self worth," our overall judgments about our worth as people, is a separate and distinct construct that is influenced by specific judgments of competence. Her evidence suggests that global self-worth is a combination of two distinct constructs: perceptions regarding "competence," how well we perform in areas we value, and "social support," the degree to which we feel that significant others acknowledge one's worth. Her studies show that children's perceptions grow richer during adolescence. By the time they reach college age, individuals can express distinct perceptions of at least twelve domains. Across the lifespan, the two most important areas of competence are physical appearance and social acceptance. The most important dimension of social support is public peer group support from classmates, peers, or coworkers (p. 80). Harter's theoretical perspective suggests that students' views of themselves are shaped by their perceptions regarding "competence." How well they think they are doing and how they view their own development depend on how they perform in areas they value and the degree to which they feel that significant others acknowledge their worth.

Ianni, F. (May 1989). Providing a structure for adolescent development. *Phi Delta Kappan,* **673–682.**

Ianni summarizes a comprehensive study of adolescents in ten U.S. communities. Based on data that spanned more than a decade, he and his colleagues report that "adolescents" are characterized by individual differences far more than they are by any "common culture" (p. 675). Results question commonly held notions such as "adolescence" as a "subculture" with values and norms that are different from the "adult" culture (p. 674). Ianni notes that, beginning with Coleman's studies of peer behavior in the 1950s, the idea that adolescent society was "unique" has been widely reinforced:

> By the 1960's we were coming to view adolescence less as one of many stages in a continuous path through life and more as a distinct and disruptive sub-society with values, norms and a culture of its own. (p. 674)

Terms such as the "generation gap" and "counterculture" reflect this perception, as do stereotypic portrayals in the media.

Ianni's findings document the importance and persistence of "diversity among communities and the effects of local differences" (p. 675). While local peer groups are certainly influential, they are inextricably linked to the adult institutions in the immediate communities. Ianni concludes that

> Despite continuing assumptions—both professional and popular—that adolescents look toward peers and away from the adult community, we found significant congruence between the world views of teenagers and those of the adults in their lives. However, such congruence means that the problems of adolescence are our problems too, and cannot be explained away by referring to a 'youth culture' that we claim adolescents invented. (p. 682)

Perhaps most importantly, Ianni's studies underscore the diversity of "adolescence." Local contexts and individual differences create tremendous variations in the experiences of adolescence. While we tend to talk about adolescence as if it were a single, unified period of life, teenagers more often experience adolescence as a number of more or less coterminous periods, each structured by such socializing environments as the family, the peer group, the work place, the media, or the criminal justice system (p. 675). Noting that individuals must often resolve conflicting messages about what adolescents are expected to do, he concludes that we need to remember that adolescents are individuals, not members of a "distinctive and age-defined caste" (p. 675).

CHAPTER-TO-CHAPTER CONNECTIONS

The preceding chapter introduced Mindful Learning as a systematic approach to promoting caring in action in the classroom. This chapter describes the ways that Mindful Learning integrates theory, research, and practice. It presents a specific planning framework for designing Mindful lessons. Two fundamental connections undergird this framework:

- Students learn best in an integrated fashion. They process information by creating personal connections with subject matter, building on emotional responses, and developing their own ways of learning.

- Successful teaching is therefore an integrative process. Good instruction reflects our knowledge of how students learn and how lessons can be organized to encourage their learning.

This chapter presents a Planning Guide that provides a framework for designing lessons and units. The chapters that follow feature specific strategies for designing lessons and offer detailed illustrations of Mindful Learning activities.

Chapter Two

Mindful Learning: Connecting theory, research and practice

Teacher:	Now that we have figured out how to determine the volume of common objects, let's see if we can figure out how to determine the volume of irregular objects. Can anyone think of a way to determine the volume of a fish?
John:	We could try to measure all of its sides and multiply it out.
Teacher:	That might be possible, but what would happen if we did that?
John:	The fish would wiggle too much.
Kathy:	I don't think we could measure a fish. There are too many surfaces.
Teacher:	How else could we try?
Danny:	We could put it in a blender, turn it on, and then pour it out.
Many voices:	Oh, yuck!
Jeff:	Wait a minute, that gives me an idea—it's like when you get in a bath tub.
Jennifer:	Yes, you could put the fish in water—that wouldn't kill it.
John:	Some kind of beaker would be better—something you could use to measure how much water it will take up. That will give us an accurate measure.
Teacher:	What will determine how much the water goes up—the volume of the fish or its weight?
Susan:	I think it will be the weight.
Mike:	I think it will be the volume.
Teacher:	How could we tell?
Jennifer:	We could set up an experiment. Use two objects.
Kathy:	Yes, ones that weigh the same but have different volumes.
Teacher:	This sounds like a good idea. Let's see if we can figure out a way to set this up for tomorrow. (Strahan, 1987, p. 19)

This classroom vignette illustrates some of the ways that teachers and students can work together to create academic connections. In this particular instance, the teacher began with a reference to the previous day's lesson and a question that connects the concepts learned with a new challenge—determining the volume of irregular objects. As the students responded with ideas, the teacher guided their inquiry toward understanding the distinctions between weight and volume as they relate to properties of displacement.

As indicated in an earlier analysis (Strahan, 1987), this vignette demonstrates how new ideas spark new connections until an "aha" moment occurs (p. 19). John's notion about the fish wiggling and Danny's joke about a blender led Jeff to create a connection. Jennifer and John extended the idea and Kathy framed a well-focused question for investigation. Encouraging such connections and "aha" moments is the essence of successful teaching. In this vignette, the teacher's questions provided a structure that guided thinking. The teacher's responsiveness to students' comments offered them the support they needed to try out ideas. While the questions were not scripted, they suggest careful planning.

Chapter one introduced the basic premises of Mindful Learning—that successful teaching integrates support and structure and that successful schools promote caring in action. Studies of Mindful Learning (Strahan, Summey, and Bowles, 1995; Summey and Strahan, 1995) have indicated that this approach can be very productive in helping students connect the ways they learn best with academic activities. This chapter presents a specific framework for designing Mindful lessons, a framework that incorporates what we have discovered about the ways students learn with specific practices from research on successful teaching.

How students learn

Learning for enjoyment

As noted in chapter one, Glasser's (1986) *Control Theory in the Classroom* provides a valuable framework for understanding why students make the choices they make. The basic premise of control theory that "we always choose to do what is most satisfying to us at the time" (p. 19) provides a clear lens for understanding classroom dynamics. Glasser suggested that one of our most powerful drives is the need to have fun, especially as fun relates to learning.

> I realize that we also learn for power, love, and freedom but to satisfy these often requires long-term dedication. It is the immediate fun of learning that keeps us going day by day, especially when we are young and have so much to learn. . . . even if all we set out to do is have fun, if we succeed, it is almost impossible not to have learned something new and often important. (p. 29)

From this perspective, the need to have fun is an essential dimension of the learning process.

Csikszentmihalyi and his colleagues (1989) insist that the most engaging state of learning is characterized by "flow." They describe "flow" as the very essence of meaningful learning.

> Flow is what people feel when they enjoy what they are doing, when they would not want to do anything else. What makes flow so intrinsically motivating? The evidence suggests a simple answer: in flow, the human organism is functioning at its fullest capacity. When this happens, the experience is its own reward. (p. 55)

The concept of "flow" is a familiar notion. All of us have had the experience of being so engrossed in reading a book or watching a movie that we lose track of time. Most of us have been so engaged with a project that we forget to take our lunch break or forget something we were supposed to do. These experiences illustrate the power of flow.

Csikszentmihalyi and his colleagues (1984) studied the daily life of adolescents over a twelve-year period. They gathered data on how participants spent their time by asking them to record events in response to beepers programmed for random intervals (p. 48). Over the course of a week, these assessments provided from thirty to fifty "snapshots of daily life" that researchers used with extended interviews to describe how adolescents viewed events in their lives. In these studies, researchers identified over one hundred different activities that adolescents viewed as enjoyable.

In a synthesis of these studies used as a basis for encouraging literacy development in the classroom, Csikszentmihalyi (1990) described some of the ways that fifth and sixth graders demonstrated "flow experiences":

One after the other, these children described what they enjoyed most about playing the piano, or swimming, or acting in the school plays. One said that while doing these things, "I can forget my problems." Another said, "I can keep the things that bother me out of my mind" and so on. In class, they claimed, they could seldom achieve such concentration. (p. 130)

Csikszentmihalyi noted that a "vicious circle" often develops in the classroom in which students are not concentrating on the tasks at hand, begin to think of other things, and then find it even more difficult to concentrate. As a result, "even in very good schools students actually pay attention to what is supposed to go on quite rarely" (p. 134). He suggested that the major barriers to cognitive engagement seem to be "external controls" through which adults impose excessive structure on students' thoughts; "evaluation" which shifts attention away from the task itself toward rewards or punishment; "competition" which shifts attention away from involvement toward attention to what others are doing; and "self consciousness" which results from fear of failure (p. 137).

Csikszentmihalyi concluded that studies of flow experiences with academic activities emphasize students' "immersion" in the tasks themselves (p. 137). Such immersion can be facilitated by teachers who "intuitively know that the best way to achieve their goals is to enlist students' interest on their side" and who "do this by being sensitive to students' goals and interests" (p. 137). He suggested that teachers play a powerful role in fostering enjoyment. They can encourage students to assume more responsibility for their own learning, offer feedback without undo attention, and nurture concentration by creating energizing climates for learning (p. 137).

> Basically, young people are influenced by adults who appear to enjoy what they do, and who promise to make youth's life more enjoyable too. This is not such a bad yardstick to use—why should youth choose models who seem miserable and who strive to impoverish their future? (p. 133)

These studies have suggested that when students are "intrinsically motivated" in classroom settings, they are finding productive ways to have fun.

This same need for enjoyment can also create distraction. When students are bored, they may create their own diversions. They may "clown around," initiate pranks, or make humorous comments. In more negative fashion, they may "poke fun" at classmates and use ridicule in attempts at humor. Any of these forms of off-task enjoyment can hamper Mindful Learning. Teachers can encourage positive expressions of enjoyment by inviting students to share their interests, offering choices, and sharing their own enthusiasm for their favorite topics and activities.

Emotional learning

While learning for fun may be the most powerful way to process information, we now understand more clearly that all learning involves feelings as well as intellect. Goleman (1995) synthesized a growing body of information on brain functioning into the concept of *Emotional Intelligence*. This concept can enrich and extend our understanding of ways students learn.

Weaving together strands of research from brain-imaging technologies and psychology, Goleman documented ways that thinking and feeling are integrated. New insights regarding emotional intelligence can help us understand the linkages between "head" and "heart" (p. xi). Goleman defined emotional intelligence as

> a set of traits—some might call it character—that also matters immensely for our personal destiny. Emotional life is a domain that, as surely as math or reading, can be handled with greater or lesser skill, and requires its unique set of competencies. (p. 36)

These competencies compliment the more traditional aspects of intelligence captured in IQ scores. Like Gardner (1983), Goleman cites a wide range of studies that chronicle the limitations of traditional measures and concludes that "at best, IQ contributes about 20 percent to the factors that determine life success" (p. 34). His analysis demonstrates that the more traditional aspects of intelligences, those characterized by the phrase "raw intellect," cannot function fully without the emotional competencies that undergird them (p. 36). More than any other aspect of thinking, emotional intelligence functions as a "meta-ability" that helps us understand and control our thoughts (p. 36).

Like other dimensions of intelligence, emotional intelligence can be difficult to describe in words or to reduce to lists of abilities. Goleman summarized studies by Peter Salovey at Yale which indicate at least five domains of emotional aptitude that function as personal intelligence:

1. **knowing one's emotions** — self awareness, monitoring one's feelings
2. **managing emotions** — self-control, builds on self-awareness
3. **motivating oneself** — channelling emotional energy and delaying gratification, another critical aspect of self-discipline
4. **recognizing emotions in others**—interpersonal awareness, empathy
5. **handling relationships**—managing emotional situations, interpersonal success, leadership. (p. 43)

These aspects of emotional intelligence are the foundation of self-discipline. Learning self-discipline requires us to know our feelings, to manage these feelings appropriately, to motivate ourselves, and to understand and respond to the feelings of others.

Understanding more about emotional intelligence provides us a stronger framework for understanding how students learn. As Goleman notes, the human brain is very different from computerized intelligence,

> in reality the brain's wetware is awash in a messy, pulsating puddle of neurochemicals, nothing like the sanitized, orderly silicon that has spawned the guiding metaphor for mind. (p. 40–41)

"Mindful" learning thus encompasses much more than concepts and ideas. Our best information suggests that the mind works from the inside out, extending self-awareness and feelings into the comprehension of other people and external realities. To teach mindfully, we need to appreciate this complexity and recognize the power of emotions. Students are most likely to learn new academic concepts when we address the "feeling tones" of information. They cannot learn self-discipline unless we do so. More than anything else, Mindful Learning is integrative. By helping students make sense out of their life experiences, Mindful Learning connects self-awareness with academic understanding.

As suggested in the first chapter, students have developed diversified views of themselves as students by the time they enter middle grades. Harter's (1990) developmental studies show that key behavioral indicators characterize young children with high self-esteem. In new settings, they actively display confidence, curiosity, initiative, and independence and they show adaptive reactions to change or stress. They are most often comfortable with transitions and can handle criticism and teasing. Young children with low self-esteem, in contrast, rarely display confidence, curiosity, initiative, or independence, and have difficulty reacting to change or stress. Moreover, their interactions with peers are more likely to be negative. Harter notes that they often have trouble playing and are more likely to be aggressive and easily offended. Harter's studies indicate that before age eight, children evaluate themselves more often in specific domains such as how well they play soccer than in more general domains such as how well they do in school.

As they get closer to the middle grades, children begin to make judgments about their personal self-worth in a more generalized fashion (Harter, 1990). In regard to school performance, students who are successful in their classes begin to assign more importance to academic self-esteem, discounting athletic success perhaps, or placing less emphasis on social competence. Students who

believe they are doing poorly in school face a difficult psychological dilemma. To feel good about themselves, they must learn to
discount the importance of academic success. For some students,
learning to believe that "school doesn't matter anyway" may be
the only way to maintain a healthy sense of self. Harter's (1988)
studies of intrapsychic conflict suggest that ninth graders are most
vulnerable to this self-defeating perception.

"Self-worth theory," as described by Covington (1984a), can
provide a useful framework for understanding how these perceptions develop. Self-worth theory suggests that "much of student
achievement behavior is best understood in terms of attempts to
sustain a reputation of competency, and hence worth" (p. 11). A
number of studies have shown that people typically try to promote positive perceptions of identity to gain approval and to min-
imize "negative social sanctions" (Covington, 1984b, p. 78). Perceptions of self-worth thus depend on interpretations of
"successes" and "failures." As many teachers have observed, students usually try to maintain a positive self-image, even when they
experience failure. For example, on the day of a test, a student
might announce that she thought the test was the next day, even as
the test papers are being distributed. Another student may sud-
denly "need" to see the nurse or "remember" he needs to go to
the office during a test. These may be strategies for saving face.

How students perceive "ability" and "effort" are also critical factors that relate to academic self-esteem. Covington (1984a) reported a number of studies that show how children in the primary grades equate ability and effort. For students in the primary grades, "trying hard" is often equated with success. As students develop more sophisticated capacities for processing information about themselves and others, perceptions of effort and ability begin change. Students in the middle grades demonstrate a much greater tendency to express views of effort and ability as "reciprocal." In many cases, they begin to attribute academic success to ability alone. Some begin to believe that "smart kids don't have to work as hard" and to view effort as an admission of lower ability.

Some school practices inadvertently encourage students to believe that "when it comes to school, I am not good enough." Competition and social comparisons seem to be key factors in the negotiation of academic selfworth. When classroom activities are primarily competitive, the risk of believing that "I am not good enough" grows greater. Covington (1984a) notes that schools often encourage students to compete for a limited number of awards. He concludes

> In effect, for every winner there must be one or more losers. This condition forces many students to abandon the positive, coping strategies associated with striving for success and to adopt tactics designed to avoid failure. (p. 15)

When students begin to view ability alone as the basis for achievement, it becomes more desirable to avoid failure and protect self-esteem than to risk thinking themselves "unable."

The desire to avoid failure can explain many of the actions of students labelled "academically at-risk." Appearing "not to try" becomes a way to avoid feeling "unable." Covington has described a number of failure-avoiding tactics: lack of effort, false efforts, procrastination, devaluation, and blaming others. Lack of effort may be a student's way of saying "I could be a good student if I wanted to." False efforts, like turning in the wrong assignment, may allow students to appear to be trying and also avoid perceptions of failure. Putting things off until the last minute, saying "it's not important anyway" or that "it is all the teacher's fault" are also familiar responses employed to avoid failure. If unchecked, these failure-avoiding tactics can become self-fulfilling prophecies and make it increasingly difficult for students to succeed. In extreme cases, students may become "failure prone," blaming poor performances on ability and attributing success to "luck," "easy work," or the "niceness" of the teacher (p. 93). Attributions such as these make it difficult for students to feel competent about themselves as students.

Self-worth theory thus provides a framework for understanding why some students grow increasingly "school weary." Again, teachers play a powerful role in creating climates that encourage students to think through some of the failure-avoiding tactics that interfere with learning. A good first step might be to accept an educator's version of the Hippocratic oath: "Be sure we do no harm." As emphasized in *Positive Discipline* (Purkey and Strahan, 1986), teachers can create more inviting climates for learning by recognizing and avoiding practices that are "unintentionally disinviting" such as excessive competition, criticism, ability grouping, or social comparisons. In this regard, personal dynamics are often most critical. Students need extra encouragement, respect, and patience. Most importantly, they need to know that their teachers care about them as individuals. That sense of caring may heighten feelings of emotional security and invite more meaningful participation.

Some students are not only weary of going to school, they openly resist learning. In recent years, research has provided detailed information about the needs of students who feel that their own personal agendas are "at odds" with the prevailing norms of their schools. Feeling "at odds" with the prevailing norms can be especially pronounced among students who see themselves as members of involuntary minorities. In his review of the literature on this phenomenon, Ogbu (1992) demonstrates that schooling influences minority students in different ways depending on the nature of their status as minorities. While schooling may create cultural and language difficulties for any student who is not a member of the privileged culture, students from "involuntary minorities" face unique obstacles in education (p. 8).

Based on a wide range of cultural studies, Ogbu describes some of the ways that "voluntary minorities" benefit over time from schooling. He defined "voluntary minorities" as "people who have moved more or less voluntarily to the United States—or any other society—because they desire more economic well-being, better overall opportunities, and/or greater political freedom (p. 8)."

He noted that students from families who have come to school under these circumstances usually expect to face challenges in learning how to go to school or to have difficulty learning the language. In many cases, they see schooling as a key to success in their new country—a means to greater power and freedom—and work to overcome these obstacles. As a rule, they do not experience "lingering, disproportionate school failure" (p. 8).

Involuntary minorities, in contrast, may experience much more difficulty in school. Involuntary or "castelike" minorities "are people who were originally brought into the United States or any other society against their will" or who were "colonized" by an invading culture (p. 8). In the United States, African American, Native American, and some Mexican American students may see themselves as members of involuntary minorities. They often face schooling practices that were developed to maintain cultural boundaries and must cope with the hidden and not-so-hidden agendas that serve to preserve privileged status. In response, they have developed "secondary cultural differences" to cope with their status, viewing certain forms of behavior and language as characteristic of "White America" (p. 8).

Ogbu noted how, over the years, African Americans have emphasized differences in style to establish and maintain a cultural identity. These differences in style manifest themselves in ways of communicating and uses of in-group language to demonstrate cultural identity. In many instances, this cultural inversion is defined in opposition to the prevailing "majority" culture.

Thus, students from involuntary minorities may consciously or unconsciously fear that by learning the "White" cultural frame of reference, they will cease to act like minorities and lose their sense of community (p. 10). This fear is reinforced as students learn that even those who learn to "act White" and succeed in school "are not fully accepted by the Whites" and do not receive the rewards or opportunities they had expected (p. 10).

Ogbu's analysis indicates that these dynamics may be especially powerful for young adolescents. As peer pressure grows more intense, involuntary minority students sometimes begin to equate success in school with "acting White."

> The dilemma of involuntary minority students, then, is that they
> may have to choose between "acting White" (i.e., adopting

"appropriate" attitudes and behaviors or school rules and standard practices that enhance academic success but that are perceived and interpreted by the minorities as typical of White Americans and therefore negatively sanctioned by them) and "acting Black," "acting Indian," "acting Chicano," and so on. (p. 10)

This tension between "acting Black" or "acting Indian" or "acting Chicano" and doing well in school by "acting White" can create powerful personal conflict for students. In many cases, this tension is viewed in oppositional terms. "Acting Black" or "acting Indian" or "acting Chicano" may mean doing the opposite of what students who "act White" do. As students grow more sensitive to these dynamics, maintaining cultural identity becomes an important dimension of self-concept and self-esteem.

If the dominant culture of the school appears White and school success is viewed as "acting White," then students may choose to resist by "acting Black," "acting Indian" or "acting Chicano" in ways that establish a contrasting identity. This resistance may include not trying, not participating, or acting disruptively. In the most extreme cases, minority students employ "encapsulation" strategies by immersing themselves exclusively in peer culture and refusing to participate in school at all (p. 11).

Ogbu's studies have documented some of the ways that involuntary minority students who want to do well in school face unique challenges. Like all students, they must learn to play the school game. They must do so without the benefit of insider information, however, and must also learn conventional study strategies and personal learning skills. At the same time, they must cope with negative peer pressure that may stigmatize them for wanting to do well. In his review of studies of students who beat these odds, Ogbu has identified a number of strategies that involuntary minority students employ to shield themselves from peer pressure. Some students choose to "act White" and experience the psychological cost of isolation from their peers (p. 11). Some employ "accommodation without assimilation," behaving according to school norms on campus and according to ethnic norms at home (p. 11). This strategy, which carries less stigma, has been described as "do your Black thing in the community but know the White man thing at school" (p. 10). Other students camouflage their success by studying in secret or becoming class clowns to mask their intentions to do well.

Ogbu has insisted that many current efforts toward core curriculum and multicultural education do not go far enough in addressing the complexity of these dynamics. Much more vigorous commitment and systematic intervention is necessary to help students understand these realities. For students to be successful, they must learn to maintain their cultural identity as they invest effort in schooling. Ogbu concluded that teachers must recognize the unique challenges faced by involuntary minorities, understand why oppositional strategies have emerged in our history, provide intensive interventions to help students separate school success from "acting White," encourage positive cultural identity and biculturalism, and work harder to improve minority status.

While the need to encourage empowerment may be especially important when working with students who perceive themselves as members of an involuntary minority, the need for more responsive instruction is critical in all classrooms. Our recent analyses of classroom dynamics demonstrate that active task resistance can be a very individualized matter (Summey and Strahan, 1996a; Summey and Strahan, 1996b). The students we observed who avoided work and resisted instruction did so for reasons they themselves may not have fully understood. Finding ways to break the negative cycle of nonparticipation requires special patience and commitment.

Much of this responsibility is personal. Earlier, we noted that students need to feel a sense of trust before they can begin to think through the academic choices they make. As difficult as it may be, teachers need to work with other teachers to identify practices that may appear to be exclusive or ineffective, consider their own personal biases or patterns of avoidance, and learn strategies that permit them to listen more openly. When they can create more trusting climates, they can find ways to tap students' talents more productively.

Multiple intelligences: An integrative theory of learning

Our analysis of ways students process information and understand new ideas underscores the complexity of learning. As teachers, we would like to be able to design lessons that encourage learning to "flow" for all of our students. We would like to plan

activities that promote self-worth and feelings of inclusion. To do this, we need an integrative framework for planning lessons and units. When we began developing the Mindful Learning framework, we found that Gardner's (1983) theory of multiple intelligences gave us a comprehensive foundation for planning lessons that can engage and challenge all of our students.

In *Frames of Mind*, Gardner (1983) demonstrates that the mind processes information in many different ways. He presents evidence from brain studies and a range of psychological investigations that documents seven recognizable "intelligences," each characterized by a pattern of neurological organization and a unique cluster of abilities. As we found in earlier analyses (Strahan, 1985; Strahan and Strahan, 1987), understanding more about these "frames of mind" can help teachers recognize and appreciate individual differences.

As Gardner indicates, most educators are very familiar with *linguistic* intelligence. His theory defines linguistic intelligence as a cluster of abilities related to verbal perceptions, expressive language, and interpretation of speech and print. He summarizes evidence that shows how literacy develops from speaking and listening, noting that "it has been established convincingly that written language "piggybacks upon oral language" (p. 87). His theory affirmed the need to help students connect what they write and read with what they hear and discuss in order to enhance their linguistic abilities.

Most educators are also very familiar with *logical-mathematical* intelligence. Gardner describes this frame of mind as a cluster of abilities related to operational reasoning, hypothetical deductive thinking, and abstract thought. Studies of "formal reasoning" have documented distinctive ways that young adolescents develop logical-mathematical understandings. For example, Piaget's conceptualization of developmental "stages" of reasoning helps illuminate logical-mathematical reasoning.

Another frame of mind that is often well-represented in descriptions of thinking development is *spatial intelligence*. Spatial reasoning involves thinking through visual perceptions and our mental representations of those perceptions. Gardner describes some of the ways that we use spatial reasoning to create mental pictures and to generate three-dimensional mental constructs.

To this familiar array of thinking abilities, Gardner adds *musical*, *bodily-kinesthetic*, *intra-personal*, and *inter-personal* intelligences. Musical reasoning involves perceiving, remembering, and expressing musical elements such as pitch, rhythm, and timbre. For some students, musical reasoning is a primary way of knowing and, for them, it is not only a powerful means of expression, but also an avenue for processing information. Bodily-kinesthetic reasoning involves the use of movement as a way of understanding. When athletes and dancers speak of "thinking through a performance," they provide glimpses of how thought can relate to motion. Students with strengths in this area need "to move to know." They need to manipulate objects to understand concepts. Intra-personal reasoning involves using an awareness of one's own thoughts and feelings to guide behavior. Inter-personal reasoning involves an awareness of the thoughts and feelings of others used as a basis for action.

Gardner and his colleagues have conducted a series of longitudinal studies of ways that children learn (Gardner & Hatch, 1989; Sternberg, Okagaki, & Jackson, 1990). They have found that all of the children they have profiled demonstrate abilities in at least one of the seven areas. At the same time, none of the children has demonstrated exceptional abilities in all seven areas. Children learn most successfully when they have opportunities to use their unique set of talents to process information. Gardner's findings underscore the complexity of individual differences. His work has encouraged educators to question traditional notions about "school smarts." Thanks to Gardner, there is a growing consensus that traditional definitions of scholastic aptitude emphasize only a narrow band of linguistic and logical performances. All children seem to benefit when a broader array of talents are nurtured.

We have found that understanding more about multiple intelligences can help teachers appreciate individual differences and begin to reconceptualize their notions of "school smarts." We have traditionally viewed "school smarts" as good reading, writing, and arithmetic. As Gardner suggests, this reflects the fact that concepts of "intelligence" are often culturally defined. Western society has traditionally valued both scientific and literary thinking. Other cultures have emphasized other dimensions of thinking. In societies of the South Pacific, as Gardner reports, individuals with exceptional spatial abilities are valued especially for their aptitude in navigation. The premiums we have traditionally placed on linguistic and logical-mathematical reasoning have resulted in a situation in which students who learn best in other ways may have less opportunity for success in school. In developing our ideas for Mindful Learning, we have tried to broaden our notion of "school smarts" to make it more likely that all students can become more academically successful through their own ways of knowing.

The response to Gardner's theory has been unprecedented. The educational community has embraced the basic notion of teaching students in ways that tap their talents. A proliferation of books and articles has offered suggestions for linking the theory to practice. Professional meetings and workshops have featured sessions on the theory.

As one might expect, this rapid progression from psychology to pedagogy has spawned both applications and misapplications. In a recent article entitled "Reflections on Multiple Intelligences: Myths and Messages," Gardner (1995) reports his analysis of these applications. In some ways, applications of theory to practice have advanced the theory itself. Gardner notes that the theory is a work in progress and suggests that he is now considering the characteristics of an "eighth" intelligence, "the intelligence of the naturalist" (p. 206). This cluster of abilities includes recognizing patterns in the world around us, understanding ways that plants grow and animals behave, discriminating among subtleties in the environment. Farmers, hunters, and naturalists excel in these abilities, as do our students who can readily identify distinctions among similar objects such as "cars, sneakers, or hairstyles" (p. 206). Gardner's analysis of ways that educators have applied and misapplied his theory stems from his own review of educational innovations.

> In the 12 years since *Frames of Mind* was published, I have heard, read, and seen several hundreds different interpretations of what MI theory is and how it can be applied in the school. (p. 202)

Based on this review, he describes seven different "myths" that have emerged, comments on these myths in reference to the research that has been conducted on multiple intelligences (MI), and offers recommendations to educators who wish to use the theory in a way that reflects the research on how students learn.

The major "myth" that Gardner addresses is that "there is a single educational approach based on MI theory" (p. 206). He emphasizes the fact that MI is a primarily a psychological theory, rather than an approach to curriculum and instruction. As a psychological theory, MI addresses ways that the human brain processes information. Some of the applications he has studied seem to miss this essential element. He addresses six practices, in particular, that reflect misinterpretations of MI learning theory:

- attempting to teach all concepts using all of the intelligences

- going through the motions of an intelligence (exercises as movement, for example)

- using learning media as background (music to study by, for example)

- using intelligences as memory aids to recitation

- confusing intelligences with teaching strategies (such as cooperative learning)

- evaluating intelligences apart from content or context. (pp. 206-207)

In highlighting these misinterpretations, Gardner reminds us that "frames of mind" are ways to understand how we process information. Musical intelligence is an aptitude for making sense of musical information such as pitch, rhythm, and timbre. Composing songs about the rainforest *might* help a student understand the rainforest better. Playing rainforest music in the background, while it might help some students read with concentration, is not musical knowing. The information processed is not necessarily musical. Likewise, pacing back and forth to enhance memorization is not bodily-kinesthetic knowing. Working in groups is not necessarily interpersonal knowing. Keeping a journal is not necessarily intrapersonal understanding.

Gardner concludes that applying an understanding of ways of knowing to improve teaching and learning requires three key elements:

1. the cultivation of desired capabilities

2. approaching a concept, subject matter, or discipline in a variety of ways.

3. the personalization of education. (pp. 207–208)

Music, movement, art, interpersonal activities, and reflection have value in and of themselves. When they correspond to concepts in the curriculum, they can greatly enrich learning, especially when teachers incorporate their understanding of individual differences. As Gardner suggests,

> I have always believed that the heart of the MI perspective—in theory and in practice—inheres in taking human differences seriously. At the theoretical level, one acknowledges that all individuals cannot be profitably arrayed on a single intellectual dimension. At the practical level, one acknowledges that any uniform educational approach is likely to serve only a minority of children. (p. 208)

No matter what instructional applications teachers may generate based on these fundamental notions of MI theory, Gardner insists that learning is a personal enterprise, suggesting

> whether or not members of the staff have even heard of MI theory, I would be happy to send my children to a school with the following characteristics: differences among youngsters are taken seriously, knowledge about differences is shared with children and parents, children gradually assume responsibility for their own learning, and materials that are worth knowing are presented in ways that afford each child the maximum opportunity to

master those materials and to show others (and themselves) what they have learned and understood. (p. 208)

Research related to multiple intelligences continues to offer new insights about how students learn.

How successful teachers teach

Based on an understanding of how students learn, Mindful Learning also incorporates a synthesis of research on instruction. The foundation for this synthesis is the growing consensus regarding factors that matter most in classroom learning. In recent years, several different teams of researchers have conducted large-scale "meta-analyses" of research reports related to student achievement. Perhaps the most comprehensive of these is the study reported by Wang, Haertel, and Walberg (1993). Their analysis of more than 11,000 relationships among variables related to achievement revealed that five categories of variables have consistently been most influential in regard to student achievement. In the order of influence, these variables are

1. classroom management,

2. metacognitive characteristics,

3. cognitive characteristics,

4. home environment/parental support, and

5. student and teacher social interactions. (p. 272)

As noted in the abstract of their study reported at the end of this chapter, any consideration of what matters most in regard to student achievement should begin with these "proximal" factors that are closest to the day-to-day events in classrooms.

As we have developed Mindful Learning, we have attempted to address all five of these essential factors. We have generated strategies for enhancing *classroom management* (see chapter four). We have designed instruction that reflects what we know about young adolescents' *cognitive characteristics* (see chapter three) and incorporated specific procedures for nurturing *metacognitive characteristics* into the planning process (see chapter three). Encouraging parental support and fostering positive student and teacher social interactions are integrated in all aspects of Mindful Learning (and summarized in chapter six). Helping students extend what they know in ways that encourage their awareness of how they know is the essence of Mindful Learning.

Other studies of successful teaching have provided us with insights that connect general patterns of teaching effectiveness with specific classroom practices. At UNC Greensboro, we have conducted a series of reviews of ways teachers "invite" students to succeed (Strahan and Van Hoose, 1987; Van Hoose and Strahan, 1992). The research-based practices that we have identified provide a strong foundation for Mindful Learning. Figure 2.1 presents a summary listing of these practices. An abstract of our research report is presented at the end of this chapter.

These practices can provide a useful starting point for examining ways that teachers can promote Mindful Learning. A more extensive analysis of successful teaching has emerged from the work of the National Board for Professional Teaching Standards (1993). In 1987 the National Board began a comprehensive analysis of research on successful teaching as a foundation for the development of the National Standards. The panel incorporated the major points of this review in issuing its five principles for *What Teachers Should Know and Be Able To Do* (1994). These principles are the foundation for all of the National Standards. Figure 2.2 lists these five principles and sixteen points of elaboration.

Figure 2.1 Mindful Learning Practices (summary form)

Planning

The teacher...

1. is prepared for class
2. has identified meaningful, thinking-centered goals for learning
3. addresses individual differences in ways of learning
4. has identified clear criteria for assessing performance
5. has incorporated opportunities for students to make choices about what to learn and/or how to learn

Presentation

The teacher...

6. begins the lesson promptly
7. provides an overview
8. uses motivating techniques to generate interest
9. speaks in a manner that facilitates student learning
10. structures the lesson in logical steps
11. makes smooth transitions between activities
12. uses personalized references for illustrations
13. uses a variety of instructional activities during a single lesson
14. summarizes the major points of the lesson

Active Involvement

The teacher...

15. provides all students an opportunity for active involvement
16. encourages students to try out ideas and take risks before "grading" performance
17. provides all students an opportunity to practice and apply new skills
18. asks varied and appropriate questions
19. asks reflective questions that stimulate thinking
20. encourages students to express personal ideas, needs, or interests
21. encourages responsibility by involving students in decision-making

Monitoring

The teacher...

22. monitors student performance to determine needs for clarification, assistance, or adjustment
23. addresses disruptions that interfere with student learning
24. responds to students with special problems
25. adjusts presentations and activities in response to feedback from students

---

Figure 2.1 (continued)

Feedback

The teacher...

26.   provides students feedback on their progress and performance

27.   praises student performance and expresses appreciation to students

28.   demonstrates support when responding to student errors

29.   gives reasons for actions, decisions, and directions

Personal Factors

The teacher...

30.   shows enthusiasm for learning and teaching

31.   communicates purposes and meaning of the lesson

32.   models courtesy and respect for students

33.   maintains patience and poise

A framework for planning

When we began our Mindful Learning project, we drafted a planning guide to help us plan lessons and units. We organized this guide to structure the planning process in a sequential fashion. Our most recent version of the planning guide incorporates the latest middle grades standards from the National Board. The Early Adolescence/Generalist Standards Committee of the National Board for Professional Teaching Standards (1993) issued a set of eleven specific standards for teaching in the middle grades. This committee of teachers and researchers based their standards on an extensive review of successful teaching practices. Their eleven standards now guide National Board assessments for the Early Adolescence/Generalist certificate. These standards provide a comprehensive summary of research on successful teaching. Figure 2.3 presents the most recent Planning Guide for Mindful Learning as they relate to the National Board Standards. Roman numerals note the number of the standard as presented by the National Board.

Figure 2.2 Guiding principles for
What Teachers Should Know and Be Able To Do
(National Board for Professional Teaching Standards, 1993)

1. Teachers are committed to students and their learning.

- Teachers recognize individual differences in their students and adjust their practice accordingly.

- Teachers have an understanding of how students develop and learn.

- Teachers treat students equitably.

- Teachers' mission extends beyond developing the cognitive capacity of their students

2. Teachers know the subjects they teach and how to teach those subjects to students.

- Teachers appreciate how knowledge in their subjects is created, organized and linked to other disciplines.

- Teachers command specialized knowledge of how to convey a subject to students.

- Teachers generate multiple paths to knowledge.

3. Teachers are responsible for managing and monitoring student learning.

- Teachers call on multiple methods to meet their goals.

- Teachers orchestrate learning in group settings.

- Teachers place a premium on student engagement.

- Teachers regularly assess student progress.

- Teachers are mindful of their principal objectives.

4. Teachers think systematically about their practice and learn from experience.

- Teachers are continually making difficult choices that test their judgment.

- Teachers seek the advice of others and draw on education research and scholarship to improve their practice.

5. Teachers are members of learning communities.

- Teachers contribute to school effectiveness by collaborating with other professionals.

- Teachers work collaboratively with parents.

- Teachers take advantage of community resources.

An illustrated analysis of the planning process

The following analysis illustrates Ms. Johnson's use of the planning guide to develop the unit that is presented in chapter one.

Figure 2.3 Planning Guide For Mindful Learning and National Standards

PLANNING GUIDE FOR MINDFUL LEARNING	EARLY ADOLESCENCE/ GENERALIST STANDARDS
1. What matters most about this topic?	**Highly accomplished generalists** draw on their knowledge of subject matter to establish goals and facilitate student learning within and across the disciplines that comprise the middle grades curriculum (II).
2. What type of connections can we create between their needs and interests and this new content?	…draw on their knowledge of early adolescent development and their relationships with students to understand and foster their students' knowledge, skills, interests, and values (I).
3. How can we encourage students to understand their personal ways of learning?	…foster students' self-awareness, self-esteem, character, civic responsibility, and respect for diverse individuals and groups (VII).
4. What type of varied activities can we develop to engage students in "hands on/minds on" learning? (How can we incorporate multiple intelligences?	…select, adapt, create, and use rich and varied resources (III).and …use a variety of approaches to help students build knowledge and strengthen understanding (VI).
5. How can we relate this topic to real-world situations and encourage problem solving?	…require students to confront, explore, and understand important and challenging concepts, topics, and issues in purposeful ways (V).
6. How will we assess learning? a. What will students do to demonstrate their knowledge? b. How can we evaluate their progress in learning concepts?	…employ a variety of assessment methods to obtain useful information about student learning and development and to assist students in reflecting on their own progress (VIII).

Background (planning guide 1 & 2)

"Human development" is a major unit in the NC science curriculum. The passage "Adolescence" in the *Integrated Science* text (Figure 1.2, page 8) provides a basic overview of some of the develop-

7. What types of concluding activities will help students integrate ideas and create new connections?	...regularly analyze, evaluate, and strengthen the effectiveness and quality of their practice (IX).
8. How can we enhance teamwork?	....establish a caring, stimulating, inclusive, and safe community for learning where students take intellectual risks and work independently and collaboratively (IV). ...work with families to achieve common goals for the education of their children (X). ...work with colleagues to improve schools and to advance knowledge and practice in their field (XI).

mental transitions that occur at this time. Middle school students may be very curious about these changes as they are experiencing them firsthand. Key concepts that connect their needs and interests with the emphases of the curriculum and text might include:

- physical growth is often uneven during adolescence and affects people in different ways

- uneven growth may result in concerns regarding one's appearance

- the onset of puberty results in emotional turbulence as well as physical changes

- adolescence is often a time of identity formation and value development

Mindful Learning activities (planning guide 3 & 4)

For Ms. Johnson's unit, students' responses to the activities checklist and classmate interview suggested that the group employed all seven frames of mind. The following activities address all seven frames of mind and encourage students to apply what they learn to their own lives:

1. Compare and contrast the images of adolescence in two music videos (musical and spatial learning). What do these sounds

and images suggest about "today's youth?" Do you think these images are accurate? What images would you suggest?

2. In small groups, brainstorm a list of ways that people change during adolescence. Create a concept map or diagram to share with the class (linguistic & interpersonal learning).

3. Read the passage "Adolescence" individually and add new concepts to the diagrams (linguistic and intrapersonal learning). List three of the major physical changes described in the passage and the accompanying emotional changes (logical learning).

4. In small groups, write two or three scenarios that portray adolescent situations. Select one of these situations to use in a game of charades with the rest of the class (linguistic, bodily-kinesthetic, and interpersonal learning).

Mindful Learning projects (planning guide 5-8)

For their grade on this unit, students may select one of the following final projects:
- Draw or sculpt a portrayal of one or more developmental changes of adolescence.
- Select a song that captures adolescent feelings and present a critique (in writing or in speech).
- Design and administer a survey about developmental transitions. Compile and analyze results.
- Analyze a short story or news report that deals with adolescence.

Expectations: Students will demonstrate one or more of the four basic concepts of the unit. "Grades" will reflect the extent to which the concepts are presented clearly and thoroughly.

This analysis indicates that the seemingly natural flow of events in lessons like Mrs, Johnson's reflect a systematic attempt to plan instruction. The Mindful Learning Planning Guide can provide a framework for designing activities that help students connect academic concepts with the ways they learn best.

Studies of Mindful Learning

Since we began the Mindful Learning project, we have conducted a series of studies. The first study (Strahan, Summey, & Bowles, 1995) chronicled two teachers' efforts to integrate Multiple Intelligences into their instruction in language arts and math. The second (Summey & Strahan, 1995) documented the responses of students with learning disabilities to a literature unit that incorporated Multiple Intelligences. The third (Summey, 1995) examined the responses of students with learning disabilities to inclusive instruction.

Case Study number one

Our first case study (Strahan, Summey, & Bowles, 1995) reported a year-long analysis of two sixth grade teachers' implementation of Mindful Learning and of their students' responses to this instruction. During the 1993–94 school year, we met with two volunteer teachers twice a month to discuss lesson plans and confer regarding data collection. We observed a total of forty lessons, occasionally assisting as co-teachers. Following observations, we recorded fieldnotes and met with teachers informally to analyze samples of students' work. A total of 129 sixth graders participated in this study, 70 students in the reading classes, 59 students in the math classes. We assessed their academic progress using *GOALS Assessments* (Psychology Corporation, 1993). At the end of the year, we interviewed a cluster sample of fifteen students to elicit their views of Mindful Learning activities.

We found that both teachers implemented Mindful Learning theory in intensive fashions. Through varied methodologies, they addressed the multiple intelligences of their students and encouraged students to reflect on ways they learned best. They developed musical enrichment activities, created movements to accompany concepts, structured group projects, and offered students a range of options for demonstrating understanding. Achievement test data suggested that their instruction was successful. Gains of almost two Grade Equivalents in reading and three Grade Equivalents in math suggested that these teachers enhanced achievement. The fact that students who began the year with the lowest achievement scores demonstrated the most significant progress suggested that these teachers were especially productive in encouraging achievement among students who had not experienced consistent success in school. Interview data suggested that the Mindful Learning activities helped students articulate their views of ways they learned best. Thirteen of the fifteen students interviewed indicated a desire to see many of the same activities occur in their classes the next year.

Case study number two

Our second case study (Summey & Strahan, 1995) documented the responses of students with learning disabilities to a literature unit that incorporated Multiple Intelligences. We focused our efforts on a seventh grade language arts classroom in which eleven identified exceptional students were placed. The exceptional students who served as the participants in this investigation were considered mildly handicapped and labeled "learning disabled" and "educable mentally handicapped." In this classroom, a language arts teacher and a special education teacher worked collaboratively to serve mainstreamed students.

To obtain information about the students and the instructional setting, we developed a case study to explore the students' perceptions of themselves and of Mindful Learning. We gathered information to profile the students' perceptions of their reading abilities, their use of reading strategies, and the type of instruction they were currently receiving. We interviewed students, used the *Flynt-Cooter Reading Inventory* (1993) to assess the students' current levels of functioning in reading, and observed lessons to identify the types of activities that teachers used in the classroom. Based on this data, we generated student profiles and collaborated with the seventh grade teachers to design a Mindful Learning unit based on the novel *The Outsiders*. We functioned as teachers and teaching assistants during this unit. We described classroom activities in detail, gathered samples of student work, and recorded students' responses to each activity. After the unit was completed, we interviewed the students to elicit their perceptions of the unit and the activities and asked students to perform a strategy for answering comprehension questions.

We found that the eleven mainstreamed students seemed to benefit from the Mindful Learning activities. They each articulated some degree of engagement with one or more of the activities. Eight of the students displayed and articulated more functional reading strategies. Six completed classroom assignments in a very proficient manner. All of them could describe certain activities in detail and explain how these activities helped them understand the novel. Our observations showed that students were more likely to participate in and complete activities that were "mindful" rather than the typical worksheets used in earlier classroom assignments. Final interviews suggested that students enjoyed activities from the Mindful Learning unit. They described skits, musical activities, and art projects that helped them learn best. Even so, three of the eleven students continued to struggle with the reading and the writing tasks assigned. These three students needed individual assistance with the study guide and the reading protocol. While they enjoyed the unit, they did not improve their reading. For these three students even the most "mindful" lessons were not really engaging. We concluded that scheduling students into mainstream classrooms did not automatically improve their engagement. While Mindful Learning provided a meaningful starting point for more successful inclusion, we realized we needed to learn more about the dynamics of inclusion.

Case study number three

Our third investigation was based on the results of the second case study showing that mainstreamed students with learning disabilities might need additional assistance in making connections between Mindful Learning activities and academic content. In a study that became her dissertation, Summey (1995) conducted an intensive analysis of instruction in two mainstreamed language arts classes during the second year of our project. This study chronicled the ways that classroom teachers collaborated with special education teachers in teaching sixth grade language arts. Pre- and post-test scores in reading and self-esteem provided a means for assessing progress in the two classrooms. As teachers taught, our research team conducted detailed observations of lesson events and examined the responses of ten students with learning disabilities who became the "focus students" of this case study. We conducted interviews with these students at the conclusion of each lesson we observed to assess comprehension individually.

Analysis of data at the end of the school year showed that reading scores improved modestly in both classes, as did perceptions of self esteem. Activities that included art, music, movement, and co-operative learning seemed to be the most engaging. Students used the language of Mindful Learning to describe ways that they learned best and were very enthusiastic about the projects they had produced. Average scores among students with learning disabilities did not rise as dramatically as did the scores of their classmates, however. Mainstreamed students in one classroom perceived their experiences more positively than did the mainstreamed students in the other. Interview responses from thirteen identified students in one classroom indicated that they felt that they had been successful and that they preferred mainstreaming to the resource room placements they had known in elementary school. While the five identified students in the other classroom indicated some degree of success, they would have preferred a resource room placement. They reported that they would like more individualized assistance.

In synthesizing her data, Summey found that four of the ten focus students improved their reading across the year and felt better about themselves as students. Observations indicated that these four students participated in instructional activities and completed assignments with little assistance. Their test scores demonstrated growth and their grades in language arts were above average. While inclusion seemed beneficial for these four students, the other six made little progress. Among these six, reading scores remained low, as did their perceptions of themselves as students.

From this third case study, we concluded that while Mindful Learning encouraged most students to become more involved in learning, we needed to develop more systematic strategies for nurturing and assessing individual performance. The diagnostic teaching and assessment strategies we developed as a result of this study are described in chapter five.

These studies indicate that Mindful Learning provides a useful framework for instructional enrichment. In all three cases, teachers incorporated art, movement, and music into their lessons more systematically than they had in years past. Observations indicated that teachers used multiple intelligences as a planning guide for selecting reinforcement activities. Average achievement scores improved and students expressed appreciation for differentiated instruction. Students seemed more aware of ways they learned and were able to use the language of Mindful Learning to talk about individual differences.

Based on these studies, participants in the Mindful Learning project have recognized a need to help students connect their learning experiences with literacy development more systematically. Learning through art, movement, and music may be even more powerful if students can use these experiences as a basis for speaking, writing, and reading with greater sophistication. This need for "articulation" suggests a learning cycle based on "experiencing, expressing, and explaining." Students might first *experience* learning through varied media, using their talents in art, music, movement, and reflection to process information and generate personal connections. Teachers might then encourage them to *express* their ideas through conversation, brainstorming, and listing activities. Once they have given voice to their ideas, students might be ready to *explain* their learning through reading comprehension and composition.

Summary

This chapter has described Mindful Learning as an evolving approach to improving instruction. Bases on studies of how students learn and how successful teachers teach, Mindful Learning offers a planning framework that links students' needs and interests with instructional strategies. The foundation for this framework is an understanding of the different ways students process information. Studies of flow theory have described how students learn for enjoyment. When they find a task personally meaningful and challenging, they learn in a natural fashion, sometimes unaware they are learning. At other times, learning may be emotionally driven. Students may process information through their feelings. Sometimes, these feelings are so strong that they are unaware that their desire to protect themselves or establish a personal identity leads to avoidance or resistance. Gardner's theory of Multiple Intelligences provides a comprehensive framework for tapping students' talents to enhance all forms of learning. The Mindful Learning Planning Guide provides a systematic framework for planning lessons that meet students emotional and academic needs. This framework reflects recent studies of successful teaching and reviews of effective instructional practices. Ways to use this framework in teaching specific lessons, working with individual students, assessing learning, and enhancing self-discipline are presented in the chapters that follow.

Classroom Applications

"Learning More About Learning Through
The Outsiders"

Purpose

These activities provide an opportunity for students to learn more about different ways of learning as they read the novel *The Outsiders*. As they read the novel, students will create personal connections with characters and events and analyze the ways characters in the novel process information.

They can then explore themes from *The Outsiders* in their own ways using "mindful learning." This series of activities can be integrated into Language Arts classes or shared as a team-wide "advisory" activity.

Core Concepts:

1. Sometimes we learn for enjoyment, that is, we read something or explore new situations because they are naturally interesting to us.

2. Sometimes we learn through our emotions. We process information based on feelings and attitudes.

3. Sometimes we learn through different types of intelligence. We may be word smart, number smart, people smart, self smart, music smart, movement smart, or picture smart.

Activities:

1. Introduce the core concepts listed above by asking students to conduct an interview with one of their classmates to find out what types of activities he or she enjoys most in the classroom as well as outside of the classroom. Students should record their responses to the following questions as a reporter would record information for a story.

1. What is(are) your favorite subject(s) in school? Why?

2. What kind of activities do you enjoy doing in the classroom?

3. What are your least favorite activities that you have to do in the classroom?

4. What extracurricular activities do you participate in at school?

5. What do you do in your spare time outside of school?

6. Do you like working in groups? Why or why not?

7. Do you like to draw or make things? Why or why not?

8. Do you enjoy activities with movement? Why or why not?

2. After recording these notes, each student should write a brief "bio" for the class that describes how his or her partner processes information.

3. Create a chart on the board that lists examples of ways classmates process information. One way to organize a chart is shown on the next page.

4. Ask students to view the movie *The Outsiders*. After the film, ask students to list examples of ways characters demonstrated different types of learning.

Learning for fun	Learning through emotions	Learning with others	Learning through art and music	Learning through movement	Learning through reading and writing	Learning through step-by-step icgic
Examples ples	Examples	Examples	Examples	Examples	Examples	Exam-

5. Ask students to select one of the major characters (Ponyboy, Johnnie, Cherrie, Dally) for a character study.

6. Ask students to work in character study groups to take notes and discuss their character as they read the novel.

7. Ask students to share highlights of their character study by presenting their project to the class. Their project might feature music, art, or drama.

8. After they have presented their project, ask students to discuss (or write) ways they expressed their own ways of learning.

RESEARCH ABSTRACTS

(summaries of three of the data-based studies referenced in this chapter as a resource for further reference and continued reading)

Ogbu, J. G. (1992). Understanding cultural diversity and learning. *Educational Researcher, 21* (8), 5–14.

Ogbu's (1992) review of research describes a number of ways that involuntary minorities develop "oppositional styles" over time as ways to cope with oppression. In some instances, adopting an oppositional style may mean "standing up to authority" and not following the "majority rules." Students behaving within this frame of reference may believe that "acting Black," "acting Indian," or "acting Chicano" means asserting independence from rules and regulations, especially if following those rules and regulations are perceived as "acting White." These dynamics become especially critical as students reach the middle grades. At this time, peer pressure to act up and act out may grow more intense. Simultaneously, students may be moving from smaller elementary schools to larger middle-level schools where "control orientations" grow more pronounced. These conflicting crosscurrents put students in the middle, caught between the school's increasing demands to "behave" and pressure from peers to "misbehave."

Wang, M., Haertel, G., & Walberg, H. (1993). Toward a knowledge base for school learning. *Review of Educational Research, 63*(3), 249–294.

Wang, Haertel, and Walberg (1993) report what may be the most comprehensive synthesis of studies related to student achievement ever conducted. Henry Levin, the editor of the *Review of Educational Research*, labeled their study "the mother of all educational research syntheses" (p. 245). The researchers examined the effects of every factor related to student achievement that they could identify. To do so, they integrated three different types of analyses. Their first analysis was an inspection of 179 reviews of research from which they identified 228 variables related to achievement. They organized these effects by category. In a second analysis, they asked the authors of these 179 research reviews to rank the variables identified and calculate mean ratings for each category. Finally, they revisited a meta-analysis originally conducted by Fraser, Walberg, Welch, and Hattie in 1987, updating this meta-analysis to include studies published since then. Their synthesis of these three analyses reflects an examination of more than 11,000 relationships.

To report their findings, Wang, Haertel, and Walberg created a category system to organize the data and analyze effects by clusters of related variables. They found that the clusters of variables that were associated most powerfully with student learning were "student characteristics" and "classroom practices." These clusters of variables were followed by two other clusters which were less powerfully associated: "home and community educational contexts" and "design and delivery of curriculum and instruction." The clusters of variables that proved weakest in association with student achievement were "school-level demographics and practices" and "state and district governance and organization" (p. 270).

The five categories of variables that were most influential in relationship to student achievement were

1. classroom management,
2. metacognitive characteristics,
3. cognitive characteristics,
4. home environment/parental support, and
5. student and teacher social interactions. (p. 272)

Wang, Haertel, and Walberg concluded that "proximal" variables, that is, those closest to classrooms, have more impact on learning than "distal" variables which affect practice at the school, district, or state level (p. 276).

Van Hoose, J. and Strahan, D. (1992). Nurturing personally and professionally inviting behaviors through a clinical supervision model. In J. Novak, (ed.), *Advances in Invitational Thinking*. Cado Gap Press.

Van Hoose and Strahan generated an instrument to use in clinical supervision based on the construct of Invitational Education. From an analysis of five major reviews of the literature on effective teaching and two published instruments for assessing teaching, they identified thirty-five practices that "invited" student success, that is, that were associated with improved performance. Initial selection criteria identified items that were documented in at least two of the reviews and one of the instruments. Descriptors for each practice provided operational definitions. A review panel of teachers and supervisors used these descriptors to analyze a videotaped lesson. Items with an inter-rater agreement of at least seventy percent were retained for the instrument. The original Invitational Teaching Observation Instrument thus represented a synthesis of research on effective teaching and the concept of Invitational Education (Purkey and Novak, 1984). The instrument consisted of thirty-two descriptors of teacher behaviors and guidelines for observing them. These descriptors were based on seven major reviews of investigations of teacher effectiveness. To connect these original descriptors with the construct of Mindful Learning, three additional syntheses of research were added to the review of literature; four additional practices were added as descriptors (items 2, 4, 5, & 16), and three of the original practices were deleted.

CHAPTER-TO-CHAPTER CONNECTIONS

The first two chapters introduced Mindful Learning as a systematic framework for encouraging achievement and promoting self-discipline. This chapter describes ways to help students understand how they learn best and presents six specific instructional strategies. Three essential connections undergird these strategies:

- Students can use the language of multiple intelligences to learn more about how they learn best.

- Teachers can plan Mindful Learning lessons that incorporate strategies that emphasize different ways of knowing.

- Whenever possible, it is helpful to offer students project options to process new concepts and new ways of knowing in an integrated fashion.

The instructional strategies described in this chapter enhance achievement, promote self confidence, and provide a base for the self-discipline strategies that are described in the chapter that follows.

Chapter Three

Promoting Academic Success

> I think about what I want to teach and I try to find an
> intelligence that would successfully tap this instructional
> activity. Instead of having students just write, they now
> draw or sing, or act it out. There are as many different
> ways to learn as there are students. Each has his/her
> own way of learning. When given areas to excel in, stu-
> dents do better using their intelligence.
>
> A. Simmons (personal communication, June 1993)
> (Strahan, Summey, & Bowles, 1996, p. 55)

Mrs. Simmons' comment addresses the essence of Mindful
Learning. As one of the original developers, she has designed a
number of ways to tap her students' talents. Mrs. Simmons agreed
to participate in our year-long study of the classroom dynamics of
Mindful Learning. Our report documents a number of ways that
she and her colleagues routinely incorporate music, art, role playing, movement, story maps, and inventive homework into their
lessons (Strahan, Summey, and Bowles, 1996, p. 55). Moreover,
they tailor activities to meet the needs of individual students.
Their success has been dramatic.

When we have shared our results in workshops at other
schools, teachers have often asked what is so unique about Mindful Learning. They note that incorporating art, music, and movement is not new. They also note that the teachers involved are dynamic individuals who have taught well all along. While all of
these observations are valid, we think that one of the most important aspects of Mindful Learning is student participation, not just
in lessons themselves, but in learning about learning.

Mindful Learning begins with students' thinking about how
they learn best and gains momentum as students begin to "own"
more of their own instruction. This chapter presents Mindful
Learning in greater detail. Once teachers are familiar with the
planning strategies presented in Chapter Two, they can begin to

plan at the lesson level. Planning for Mindful Learning begins with students' explorations of ways they learn best.

Helping students understand how they learn best

Over the past five years, teachers have generated a variety of strategies for introducing the concept of multiple intelligences. Many have colorful bulletin boards with the seven types of "smart." Some have developed skits for demonstrating the types of learning. Several have involved students in interviewing each other. One team encouraged students to prepare a videotape describing their learning patterns to their parents.

Self awareness activities. All of us have employed a few common surveys and checklists. During the first year of the project, we developed a packet of nine different paper-and-pencil activities for every advisory group in the school. The following two activities proved especially useful.

Figure 3.1 Survey of Learning Choices: Self-Awareness Through Mindful Learning My Learning Choices

Directions: Read each activity listed below and choose ONE answer that best describes what you would do in the situation described. Put your answer in the space provided.

_____1. Suppose you just bought a new bike that has to be put together. Which of the following choices would you prefer to do?
   a. read the directions and put the bike together yourself
   b. get your parents or a friend to help you put it together
   c. spread out the pieces and just put it together
   d. take the bike back to the store and pay someone to put it together

_____2. Suppose you could go visit another country over the summer, but you need to find out some information about the people, their way of life, the climate, etc. Which way would you prefer to learn about the country?
   a. go to the library and check out books about the country
   b. watch a video tape about the country
   c. try to find someone who has lived in the country or visited the country so you can talk to him or her about it
   d. write a letter to a travel agency asking for information about the country

_____3. If you had some baseball cards and you wanted to know how valuable they were, what would you rather do to find out?
   a. visit a baseball card store and take your cards so you can discuss with the people who work there
   b. look in a book that gives the values of cards
   c. write a letter to the baseball company and ask if they can send a list
   d. use a computer program that is linked to a network that keeps up-to-date information on baseball cards

_____4. Suppose you want to learn a new set of fitness exercises. How would you prefer to get started?
   a. join a group where everyone is learning how to do the exercises
   b. buy a book about the exercises and learn how to do it yourself
   c. watch a video that explains these exercises
   d. observe other people briefly and try it yourself

_____5. You have to do a special project for your science class about the solar system. Which type of project would you rather do?
   a. write a song that tells something about the nine planets. It can be an original song or rap, or it can be made up to the tune of a popular song or rap
   b. build a model or draw a picture that shows the size and relationship of the planets
   c. make up a play in which each person is a planet and act it out for the class
   d. collect data about the distance each planet is from the sun and make a chart that gives this information

Figure 3.1 Survey of Learning Choices *continued*

_____6. Your class is studying pollution and the teacher wants some ideas for trying to control the problems caused by different types of pollution. Which would you choose to do?
   a. write about what you think would be helpful in a journal for the teacher to read later
   b. get into groups to discuss solutions and have one person record the ideas to share with the class
   c. make a video or cassette tape of your ideas to present to the teacher or class
   d. interview other people to get their opinions about possible solutions

_____7. Your teacher has decided to try something new in class. At the beginning of each class, you will be doing a quick warm-up activity before class starts. Which type activity would you prefer to do?
   a. putting together some type of puzzle
   b. trying to solve a short mystery the teacher reads aloud
   c. having a different student each day act out a different word or phrase for the class to guess
   d. writing in a personal journal

_____8. If you had to memorize something for a test, which of the following things would you be most likely to do?
   a. read it over and over
   b. say it out loud over and over
   c. write it out over and over
   d. make up a song or a saying to help you remember
   e. make mental pictures as a way to remember

_____9. You have a list of vocabulary words to learn for social studies class. Your teacher gives you a choice of activities. Which would you prefer to do?
   a. make a collage or use pictures that represent the words
   b. write a creative story that uses as many of the words as possible
   c. make up a word puzzle that uses the words
   d. work in groups to make up a game to help learn the words

_____10. You have a chance to go to a special summer camp. Which type of camp would you prefer to attend?
   a. computer camp
   b. arts and crafts camp
   c. some type of music camp for singing or for playing musical instruments
   d. some type of sports camp where you learn about whatever sport interests you

Figure 3.2 Mindful Learning Rating Scale
Self-Awareness Through Mindful Learning
Project Activity Rating Scale

Directions: For the next set of questions, pretend that your teacher is doing a unit on adolescent growth and development. She has asked you to select what type of project activity you would like to do. She will then divide the class into study teams based on their choices. Please use the following scale to rate the projects:

1—I would definitely choose this
2—I might choose this
3—I would not choose this (if I could help it)

_____ 1. Reading in the library and making note cards on facts about physical growth.

_____ 2. Writing mini-booklets about growing up for other students to read privately.

_____ 3. Working on a survey of how students in your grade feel about "growing up."

_____ 4. Drawing graphs and making posters showing growth changes for boys and girls during middle school.

_____ 5. Looking for pictures from magazines to illustrate ideas about "today's youth."

_____ 6. Taking pictures with a camera to illustrate ideas about "today's youth."

_____ 7. Finding music to fit your ideas about "today's youth."

_____ 8. Interviewing older students about their memories of middle school.

_____ 9. Making video clips from TV show on "today's youth."

_____10. Writing letters to students in other countries about "today's youth."

_____11. Working with other students to create dances that represent "today's youth."

_____12. Acting out situations that show "today's youth."

Questions

1. Of these twelve activities, which two would be your top selections? Explain why.
2. When you think about the activities you have selected, would you rather work by yourself or with others?
3. Would you like to do a unit like this in your class? Why or why not?

Group process activities. Students' responses to these paper-and-pen-cil activities have helped us introduce the language of multiple intelligences. Using terms like "body smart" and "picture smart" helps students internalize concepts of learning. The most important aspects of this introduction, however, are students' awareness of their own ways of knowing and their appreciation for the differences among their classmates. Our most engaging and productive activities have gone beyond the paper-and-pencil routine to promote dialogue.

One of the best ways we have found to promote discussion is the "classmate interview" activity (Figure 3.3). Using this frame-work as a point of departure, teachers have generated many variations on this theme.

While students often have a general understanding of what it means to be "music smart" or "word smart," some of them may not have fully experienced some of the ways of knowing. We have found that one of the most productive ways to encourage students to reflect on how they learn best is to begin with structured "mini-lessons" that emphasize one specific way of knowing and then ask students to analyze their own personal responses to this type of ac-tivity. The two mini-lessons that follow illustrate ways teachers can structure these types of experiential discussions.

Bodily-kinesthetic mini-lesson: "Traveling in the Milky Way"

This activity will enhance students' understanding of kinesthetic learning. While all students benefit from learning through mov-ing, some students find concrete learning experiences a neces-sity. This mini-lesson will offer students a structure for "moving to learn" and will guide them in thinking about how helpful this type of lesson activity is to them. It will take 15–20 minutes and will require a yellow ball to represent the sun.

1. Briefly explain what it means to learn kinesthetically (to learn through movement, learning to move and moving to learn). Ask students to describe examples from sports or dance. Ask them, "What is the difference between putting a movement into play and thinking through movement?"

Figure 3.3 Classmate Interview: Self-Awareness Through Mindful Learning—Classmate Interview

Directions: Interview a classmate to find out what types of activities he or she enjoys most in the classroom as well as outside of the classroom. Write in the responses in the spaces below.

1. What is your favorite subject(s) in school? Why?

2. What kind of activities do you enjoy doing in the classroom?

3. What are your least favorite activities that you have to do in the classroom?

4. What extracurricular activities do you participate in at school?

5. What do you do in your spare time outside of school?

6. Do you like working in groups? Why or why not?

7. Do you like to draw or make things? Why or why not?

8. Do you enjoy activities with movement? Why or why not?

2. Assign students to represent each of the planets in our solar system (Mercury, Venus, Earth, Mars, Jupiter, Saturn, Uranus, Neptune, Pluto). Ask a tall student to be Jupiter, a small-framed student to be Pluto, etc.
3. After each planet has been assigned, place the yellow ball in the center of the room and ask all students to arrange themselves according to distance from the sun.
4. Ask two students to represent the rings of Saturn.
5. Ask the remaining students to be the asteroid belt (which separates the inner and outer planets and is located between Mars and Jupiter).
6. Ask these students to take their place and form a distinct circle by holding hands (if possible). Once the students are in place have the planets begin rotating around the sun.
7. Ask the Earth to rotate on its axis as it moves around the sun.

This exercise will reinforce the names of the planets, the relationship between distance from each planet to the sun, the order of the planets, and the area (asteroid belt) that separates the inner and outer planets.

Reflections

At the end of this activity guide students in a discussion of how they felt about this activity. Ask them if they now have a better understanding of how the planets are arranged and move. Did they enjoy this type of activity? Then ask the students if they have a better feel for what kinesthetic learning is and how this activity compares to other kinesthetic activities they have experienced. Finally, ask students to rate their own preference for kinesthetic learning.

Spatial learning mini-lesson: "Vocabulary illustrated"

The following activity provides a systematic strategy for connecting vocabulary terms with visual images. This activity will enhance the students' understanding of visual learning.

1. Write 20–30 vocabulary words with brief definitions on 3 x 5 cards (one per student).
2. Shuffle the cards and deal them to students.
3. Briefly explain what it means to learn visually (to learn through pictures and images). Ask students to describe examples. Ask them, "What is the difference between seeing pictures someone else has made and thinking with your own mental pictures?"
4. Ask each student to draw a picture depicting his or her word.
5. When students have completed their illustrations, ask them to share their picture and explain what it depicts. Alternatively, hold up each card and ask the class to guess which word the picture is depicting.
6. Use the original cards to give a "quiz."

Reflections

Upon completing this activity, ask students to reflect upon how they learned through pictures. Start the discussion by asking them to grade their quiz and analyze the ways they remembered. Ask students for input on how to improve this activity and how to relate it to other subject matter. Do some students relate to this activity better than others?

After students have had an opportunity to experience a particular type of learning, teachers can ask them to reflect on how well that particular type of activity helped them understand the content. Figure 3.4 provides a sample survey to structure this information.

No matter how teachers have decided to introduce the concept of multiple intelligences and the languages of learning, all agree that it is important for students to have an opportunity to organize and record information for themselves. Figure 3.5 (page 79) presents two samples of student notes on multiple intelligences.

The first portion of this chapter emphasized the importance of student participation in Mindful Learning—not just active involvement, but learning about learning. The notes in Figure 3.5 indicate that Thomas and Amanda have recorded the basic terms of multiple intelligences and related them to their own experiences. This awareness sets the stage for students to examine learning strategies more specifically.

Figure 3.4 Student Survey For Mini-Lessons

TOPIC: _____

INTELLIGENCE USED:_____

Directions: Please help us plan future activities. Circle a response for each question.

1. Did this activity help you think about ways of learning?
       Yes   No   Maybe so

2. Before this activity, did you realize that this was a way of learning?
       Yes   No   Maybe so

3. Would you like to see your teachers use this type of learning in your other classes?
       Yes   No   Maybe so

4. Do you think you learn best this way?
       Yes   No   Maybe so

5. Do you understand this way of learning well enough to explain it to your peers?
       Yes   No   Maybe so

Please write two or three sentences that tell us what you think of this type of activity and how it works for you:

Teaching Mindfully

The Planning Guide for Mindful Learning presented in Chapter Two offers a wide range of possibilities for designing varied activities across units of instruction. At the lesson level, we have found that a set of recurring strategies can help students understand how they learn best and can guide us in tapping their talents as we teach content topics. The section that follows presents a sample of the strategies we have found most helpful in combining instruction and diagnosis. Each of these strategies has been well researched and reflects a distinct way of knowing.

Figure 3.5 - Student Notes On Multiple Intelligences

Thomas Ragsdale
MRS. SIMMONS, 6th grade

! DON'T EVER THROW THESE NOTES AWAY !

1.) Verbal/Linguistic (Word smart)

—good writers   —readers   —speakers
—good overall communication

2.) Musical Rhythmic (Beat smart)

—play instrument   —need a beat to concentrate

3.) Logical/mathematical (math-problem smart)

—organization   —reason out things
—follow a path

4.) Visual/Spatial (Art smart/creative smart)

—artistic   —lots of detail
—great imagination   —doodler

5.) Bodily/Kinesthetic (moving smart)

—move to learn   —science labs
—play sports   —always active

6.) Intrapersonal/Single Smart

—work alone   —control own emotions

7.) Interpersonal/People Smart

—always part of team or group   —understand others
—enjoy working with others
—love to socialize

Using Artifacts—Conscious Comprehension Through Manipulatives

As long as there have been lessons, there have probably been manipulatives. It is not difficult to imagine teachers in ancient times using stones to teach counting or natural objects to teach

Amanda Hall
9/18/95

I have four main multiple intelligences. They are word smart, math smart, art smart, and single smart. I'm word smart because I'm a good writer and a good reader (Ex. 1). I'm math smart because I'm organized, I like to follow a path, and I like to reason out things (Ex. 2). I'm art smart because I'm artistic, I have a great imagination, I like detail, and I often doodle (Ex. 3). I'm single smart because I like to work and be alone, I understand myself, and I control my emotions (Ex. 4).

Ex. 1 I've read over 100 novels.

Ex. 2 All of my books are alphabetized.

Ex. 3

Ex. 4   I am shy so I can't and hate to work in groups.

letters. Providing students with concrete materials to explore abstract concepts remains a hallmark of good teaching.

Potter and Hannemann (1977) present a systematic strategy for linking manipulatives and concepts. Entitled "Conscious comprehension: Reality reading through artifacts," their strategy presents a step-by-step method for helping students connect their observations of concrete objects with inferences they make about ideas. Their strategy proceeds as follows:

1. The first step is to identify key concepts in a text passage and prepare a cluster of "artifacts" that relate to that passage. In the example that follows, the text passage describes objects

used in bartering systems. We gathered arrowheads, coins, jewelry, precious stones, furs, and fruit.

2. The teacher begins the lesson by asking students to examine a set of artifacts. We find it helpful to divide the class into several small groups, assign group recorders, and direct students to list descriptive terms as they examine each of the artifacts.

3. After each student has had an opportunity to study each of the artifacts, the teacher asks each group to write a statement that connects the artifacts in some form of generalization.

4. When these statements are complete, the teachers asks the students to list the "inferences" they have made in writing this statement and relate these inferences to the specific objects they examined.

5. As this discussion progresses, the teacher asks students to compare logical inferences that "fit" their objects with any "wild guesses" they have made.

6. At this point, the teacher introduces the text passage and asks students to examine the text data as they did the artifacts.

7. The teacher again asks students to take notes, listing inferences and making predictions

8. The teacher again asks students to compare logical inferences with wild guesses and to describe their thought processes.

The following lesson on "monetary systems" demonstrates the use of this model and illustrates these steps:

Topic: The history of money

Goals:
1. Students will integrate information from their study of historical periods as it relates to ways people lived and ways monetary systems have evolved.
2. Students will explore the concept of "medium of exchange" by working together to develop bartering systems.
3. Students will make predictions about patterns of economic evolution and answer "think and search" questions to test their predictions.

Materials: artifacts for bartering simulation (arrowheads, coins, jewelry, precious stones, furs, fruit) passage entitled "The history of money" (Figure 3.6)

Activities:

1. Present lesson overview. Explain that the topic, "the history of money," will be used to integrate information from sixth grade social studies. The task will be to review how our monetary system has evolved and to predict what may happen in the future.
2. Explain "bartering" simulation. Each group will study a set of "artifacts," develop a system of exchange, and "trade" with another "tribe." Each tribe will have one type of item to trade. Each tribe will try to obtain at least one of each item.Teachers should guide this inquiry by asking questions such as:
   • Which of these items would be worth the most to people in ancient times?
   • Why?
   • How would you trade fruit for tools? Furs for precious stones? (go through all combinations)
   How would you develop a "system" for barter?
3. Tribes will now try to trade with each other to see how much "value" they can accumulate. Each tribe will report its "inventory" and describe how it gained wealth.
4. Discuss the simulation, asking questions such as:

- What did you learn about barter?
- Why did some items become more valuable?
- What do we mean by "medium of exchange?"
- How did our monetary system evolve?

5. Ask groups to test their predictions by reading the passage "Money."

Figure 3.6 "The History of money"

Adapted from McWilliams, L., & Rakes, T. (1979). *Content Inventories.* DuBuque, Iowa: Kendall-Hunt.

Since ancient times, people have exchanged goods and services using a system of **barter**. Barter means trading something for something else. A family with lots of furs might trade a few furs for extra fruit, for example. Bartering occurs when someone has a **surplus** of goods that someone else wants. Trading goods and services with barter is often difficult, however. People who want to trade have to find other people who have what they want and who want to trade with them. Deciding how much one product is worth may also be a problem. A person with extra fruit would have to decide how much fruit to trade for a fur, and so on.

As trade grew more common, people soon developed the idea of **medium of exchange**. They found that common products could be used as bases for trading. Over the years, many different items have been used this way: animal teeth, furs, beads, shells, tools, etc. As metals became more available, many societies began to use metal as a medium of exchange. Sometimes they used little pieces. Sometimes they weighed out lumps or dust. Over time, people learned to stamp pieces of metal into standard shapes and sizes and invented **coins**. Historians have found records of coins as early as 700 B.C. By the time of the Roman Empire, coins were common. As a monetary system, coins made trade much easier. They provided common values for exchanges, were easy to transport, and could last a long time.

Paper money first appeared in China in about the tenth century. It was not used much until the 1600s. For a long time, paper money was an individual unit, someone's promise to pay a certain amount to someone else. Even though it was easier to carry than gold, paper money did not become widespread until the 1900s. During the Civil War, the United States government began issuing its own paper money. At first, these notes were "promises" for the government to pay a certain amount in gold. Now, paper money has value because it has become part of our society.

In recent years, people have begun to use other mediums of exchange. Bigger banks have made it possible for people to write **personal checks**. Checks allow people to transfer money from their account to another. Computers have made this process even faster and have made it possible to use **credit cards**. Credit cards allow people to purchase products now and pay later. Many people believe that computers will soon handle almost all exchanges of money. This type of monetary system will be very different from bartering.

6. Review responses and discuss conclusions, asking questions such as:
   - What do we mean by "medium of exchange?"
   - What were some of the patterns in the evolution of money?
   - How does the type of money people use reflect their values?
   - What does our monetary system suggest about our values?
   - What will monetary systems be like in the future?

Potter and Hannemann's (1977) original strategy has proven to be a powerful framework for helping students understand how they can move to learn. Recent studies by Sowell (1989) in mathematics and by Rubin and Norman (1989, 1992) in science have demonstrated that using manipulatives in a structured fashion improves student achievement.

Decision Making—An Approach to Learning Logically

Another well-established strategy is the use of problem-solving frameworks to encourage logical decision making. Teaching the "scientific method" in a step-by-step fashion has long provided a means for helping students think through the process of experimental reasoning.

Durrant, Frey, and Newbury (1991) developed a systematic strategy for linking basic steps in problem solving with analysis of real-life situations faced by young adolescents. Using the acronym D-E-C-I-D-E, their strategy presents a step-by-step method for helping students define problems, generate options, and evaluate consequences. In our curriculum development on decision making (Strahan, Nadolny, Potter, and Jones, 1993), we adapted their strategy as follows:

1. Ask students to list (on the board) challenging decisions that middle school students must make.
2. Select one of these decisions and ask a student to describe how he or she thinks through this decision (list steps on the board).
3. Introduce a poster with the D-E-C-I-D-E steps listed as follows:
   Describe the problem.

Explore to identify different solutions to the problem.
Consider the consequences of each solution.
Identify the best solution.
Do it!
Evaluate your decision and learn from what happened.
(Durrant, Frey, and Newbury, 1991, p. 207)

4. Ask students to compare the steps listed on the board for the decision described with the steps in D-E-C-I-D-E.
5. Read an excerpt from a work of realistic fiction that portrays a character making a decision.

[A good example is the excerpt from *Izzy, Willy Nilly* (1986) by Cynthia Voigt that is presented in Durrant, Frey, and Newbury (1991) on pages 210–211. In this passage, Izzy attends a party after a football game. As a sophomore, she is delighted to be invited by Marco, a senior. At the party, Marco spends most of his time drinking with his friends. When it is time to go home, Izzy is not sure what to do. She has to decide whether or not to let Marco drive her home. When Tony offers to drive her home, Izzy worries that there may be a fight. She decides to let Marco drive her home. He loses control of his car and hits a tree. Izzy is badly injured and loses her leg.]

6. Ask students to work with a partner to map out the ways the character in the story thinks through the decision (in this example, how Izzy decided what to do).
7. Create a group map of the decision.
8. Ask students to critique the decision and suggest alternatives.

Figure 3.7 shows how a group of sixth graders analyzed the decision-making processes Izzy employed in this example and documents the alternatives they suggested.

This type of logical decision making lesson is a powerful way to introduce a framework for systematic problem solving. Students can then use this framework to analyze decisions made by characters in other stories, by historical figures, by scientists, or by mathematicians. Once they are familiar with this strategy, they can analyze real-world situations in which they must think through the choices they make and process these choices in writing, discussion, or debate.

Garnett and Bullock (1991) found that a using systematic strategy like D-E-C-I-D-E helped sixth graders improve both gen-

eral problem solving and mathematical reasoning. In our pilot study (Strahan, Nadolny, Potter, and Jones, 1993), we found that students learned to analyze decision scenarios more systematically and reported a greater tendency to apply this framework to some of their own difficult decisions.

Creating Graphic Organizers—Tools to Enhance Visual Learning

Creating graphic organizers to show students the relationships among essential concepts and key terms in a text passage is another well-established instructional strategy. Teachers have used this strategy for years. It has become so widespread that many publishers have incorporated graphic organizers into the structure of their textbooks.

Irvin (1990) defines graphic organizers as "means by which relationships between words can be shown in the form of a diagram"

Figure 3.7 Sample "Decision Chart" For *Izzy, Willy Nilly*

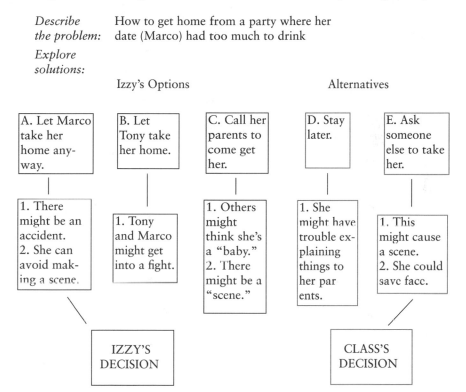

Describe the problem: How to get home from a party where her date (Marco) had too much to drink

Explore solutions:

Izzy's Options   Alternatives

A. Let Marco take her home anyway.

B. Let Tony take her home.

C. Call her parents to come get her.

D. Stay later.

E. Ask someone else to take her.

1. There might be an accident.
2. She can avoid making a scene.

1. Tony and Marco might get into a fight.

1. Others might think she's a "baby."
2. There might be a "scene."

1. She might have trouble explaining things to her parents.

1. This might cause a scene.
2. She could save face.

IZZY'S DECISION

CLASS'S DECISION

(p. 85). Irvin cites a review of research by Moore and Readence (1984) that found that graphic organizers improve performance on vocabulary tests, especially when students create their own graphic organizers rather than merely use those prepared by the teacher (p. 85). In a study designed specifically to assess science learning in the middle grades, Hawk (1986) found that sixth and seventh graders who used graphic organizers across a semester remembered more science content than did a comparison group who completed all of the same activities except the graphic organizers (see Research Abstracts).

Graphic organizers seem to be a natural strategy for students who learn well visually. By combining words and pictures in a structured fashion, graphic organizers can help students link images and ideas. A general procedure for creating graphic organizers is as follows:

Figure 3.8 Sample Graphic Organizer

Uneven Growth

Worried Looks

TRANSITIONS OF ADOLESCENCE

Changing Feelings

New Values

1. Identify important words and ideas from a text passage or from lecture notes.
2. Arrange terms on a poster board or transparency in a way that reflects the relationships among them.
3. Add illustrations and/or artwork to provide a visual reference for each of the terms.
4. Guide students in using the Graphic Organizer as an introduction to ideas and a review of information.
5. Whenever possible, encourage students to construct their own graphic organizers as study notes or presentations.

Figure 3.8 presents an example of a graphic organizer for the text passage on "Adolescence" used in chapters one and two.

Developing Book Clubs—A Structure for Shared Reading

The Book Club concept is another familiar strategy. The basic notion of sharing a book with two or three other readers has been part of the daily routine of schooling for a long time. In recent years, studies of literacy development have helped teachers structure this comfortable routine into a more systematic framework for encouraging understanding.

Raphael and McMahon (1994) describe this approach as an integration of Book Club discussion groups, community sharing sessions, reading, writing, and strategy instruction (p. 104). They define the "clubs" as "groups of three to five students mixed on several traits (e.g., gender, ethnicity, reading ability), who discuss ideas related to the books they read" (p. 104). In a series of classroom studies, they developed the following general procedures for implementing Book Clubs.

1. Select a theme and identify a set of good books to introduce the concept of the Book Club.
2. Structure a discussion of the differences between answering questions about comprehension and having a conversation about a book. Practice having conversations. Encourage good listening and clear communication.
3. Show students options for making entries in their reading logs. Options might include
   a. creating a character map that shows how they think characters look and what they do,
   b. making a sequence chart of events,
   c. listing words they find interesting,
   d. drawing pictures of what they see in their heads when they read, and writing about their pictures,
   e. making notes about the author's craft,
   f. writing about their reactions to part of the story (p. 109).
4. Organize students into clubs (mixing gender, ethnicity, reading ability).

5. Introduce the text(s) to be read. If using more than one book, present brief "book talks" on each selection and help the clubs select their choice(s).
6. Schedule times for reading, writing, and group sharing. Community share sessions can provide a setting to introduce ideas to the class or to encourage students to share issues/reactions from their reading.
7. Sit in on discussions to facilitate conversation and monitor students' use of reading strategies.
8. Plan strategy instruction sessions to teach reading skills. Instructional sessions might feature word recognition strategies, comprehension strategies, role playing, or dramatizations.

Raphael and McMahon (1994) report a series of studies that have documented ways that the Book Club approach has proven beneficial (p. 115). They note that students who have participated in Book Clubs have made as much progress on standardized tests as have students who received traditional reading instruction. Moreover, Book Club students could recall much more about their reading when questioned at a later date. Book clubs enhanced individual growth in reading, progress in writing, and the quality of group discussions,

While designed to be used in literature classes, we have found that the Book Club approach can be used with almost any subject area. We have found this approach especially effective when a team of teachers works together to teach a strategy. For example, we have used Book Clubs to enrich "test taking" preparation. We began by forming Book Clubs to read selections from a set of "high interest/low vocabulary" paperbacks using the procedures suggested by Raphael and McMahon (1994). We then introduced mini-lessons to teach the following general strategy (Figure 3.9, Five S.M.A.R.T. Steps To Reading Test Passages).

We showed students how to use this strategy to answer the comprehension questions that accompanied their books. Encouraging them to work together gave them practice in recognizing topics, identifying questions they could look up, selecting key words, and using process of elimination. The Book Club format gave us a natural setting for "modeling" these strategies as groups finished reading the chapters in their books. Once students were

---

Figure 3.9 Five S.M.A.R.T. Steps to Reading Test Passages

1. Skim the test passage and the questions.
   - Think what the passage is about.
   - See what the questions want you to know.
2. Mark the questions.
   - Circle "key words" in the question.
   - Put a ✓ beside the questions you think you can answer by finding information in the passage that is "right there."
3. Answer all the questions with a ✓ first.
4. Read to find the answers to the "right there" questions.
   - Look for "key words".
   - Cross out answers that do not make sense.
5. Think and search for answers for the rest of the questions.
   - Use all of the time you have.
   - Make good guesses.

* Adapted from Vaughn, J. and Estes, T. (1986). A self-monitoring approach to reading and thinking (SMART) in *Reading and reasoning beyond the primary grades*. Boston, MA: Allyn and Bacon.

---

familiar with these strategies, we planned lessons that incorporated the SMART steps with passages from math, science, and social studies. By starting with books that they could read comfortably and weaving the SMART strategies into Book Club discussions, students gained confidence in answering questions like those they find on many types of tests.

Cooperative Learning—Teams that Foster Interpersonal Learning

Perhaps the most widespread approach to encouraging students to learn to work together as they process new information is cooperative learning. As Walberg (1995) notes

> With justification, cooperative learning has become widespread in American schools. Not only can it increase academic achievement, but it has other virtues. By working in small groups, students learn teamwork, how to give and receive criticism, and how to plan, monitor, and evaluate their individual and joint activities with others. (p. 17)

Walberg notes that more than fifty studies have shown positive effects from cooperative learning (p. 17).

Gabel (1995) reviewed twenty-eight of the studies as they relate to achievement in science. She concludes that cooperative learning, especially when structured in "jigsaw" fashion, improves achievement in science at all grade levels (p. 125). Among the benefits cited are increased achievement scores, long-term retention, more positive attitudes toward schoolwork, higher self-esteem, higher skill achievement, and more time on task (p. 125).

While cooperative learning takes many forms, the general "jigsaw" procedures Gabel describes are as follows:

1. Assign students to groups of four in a way that mixes ability levels and familiarity with the subject. These groups will serve as "home teams" for the lesson. Once they have developed a work plan, members of the "home team" will select one of four research groups ("expert" groups) to gather information.
2. Assign roles within each group (recorder, checker, facilitator, materials coordinator, etc.) These roles will rotate across the unit.
3. Divide the content to be covered into four focus areas (topics, time periods, functions, etc.) to be covered by the four "expert" groups.
4. Ask each group to decide who will join each of the four expert groups.
5. Structure the assignments so that each of the four expert groups is accountable for specific tasks.
6. Guide each of the expert groups in studying its topic.
7. When expert groups have completed their tasks, ask each expert to teach his or her topic to the home team.
8. Structure a synthesis task that fosters competition among the home teams.

Gabel found that cooperative learning fosters group interdependence and individual accountability as well as experience with group processing. Following an overview of "multimedia learning" in the next section, a description of a unit on Native American Research will provide an illustration of cooperative learning as well as the use of multimedia.

Multimedia Projects—Linking Visual, Musical, and Linguistic Learning

As instructional technology has grown more sophisticated, teachers have developed a wide variety of strategies for encouraging students to connect visual, musical, and linguistic learning. No longer are project presentations restricted to silent sets of pictures, songs with lyric sheets, or "show and tell."

One of the many technological tools available to support students in integrating information and media is HyperStudio (Roger Wagner Publishing, Inc., 1993–94). HyperStudio is a software package that allows students to combine text passages with sounds, pictures, and videos. They can write their own passages, record their own sounds/music, input their own drawings, create computer graphics, or import published graphics. Barron (1994) found that using tools such HyperStudio promotes critical reasoning processes such analysis, sequencing, synthesis, and evaluation as well as creativity. When combined with cooperative learning, assignments can foster teamwork and integration of ideas. Means and Olson (1994) found that classrooms that employed technology most successfully shared five key features:

1. An authentic, challenging task is the starting point for projects. Students view these tasks as meaningful.
2. All students participate in activities requiring higher level thinking and reasoning.
3. Students work in heterogeneous, collaborative groups.
4. Teachers function as coaches, providing support and structure for student performance and reflection.
5. Students work over extended periods of time. (pp. 17–18)

To connect research and practice, Lisa Allen, a fourth-grade teacher and graduate student at UNC Greensboro, designed a strategy for using multimedia with research reports. As her students used HyperStudio in completing their investigations into Native American culture, Allen (1996) examined their patterns of motivation and content learning. She found that this approach increased students' intrinsic motivation as well as their understanding of Native American culture. The general strategy she developed is as follows:

1. Develop a planning guide for researching the content. Figure 3.10 presents the planning guide for the Native American unit.
2. Assign students to groups and assist them in completing their research.
3. Develop a rubric for assessing content learning and Hyper-Studio projects. Figure 3.11 presents Allen's rubric.
4. While students are working in their research groups, introduce a series of lessons demonstrating how to use the navigational tools of HyperStudio.
5. When students have completed at least half of their research, show them how to create "storyboards," a paper-and-pencil arrangement of text fields, pictures, buttons, backgrounds and clip art. Students can begin to experiment with arrangements and create layouts to guide the preparation of stacks.
6. Assist students in writing and revising their text fields, incorporating information from their research and returning to research to fill in gaps.
7. Continue to demonstrate new navigational tools for Hyper-Studio.
8. As students complete their projects, provide time for them to present their stacks to classmates. Assist them in using the rubric to assess their work.

It is difficult to capture students' expression of ideas using Hyper-Studio in a text format like this. The final Native American projects that students created included written summaries of the information they found in their research, artwork they had created themselves, and musical excerpts to demonstrate folkways. They presented all of this with computer animation and sound effects. These presentation modes allowed them to create their own unique blends of visual, musical, linguistic, and logical learning. In working together and independently, they extended interpersonal and intrapersonal knowing. Creating story boards using cutouts and manipulatives involved kinesthetic knowing. The integration of all of these experiences creates products that can be used as teaching tools.

Figure 3.10 Planning Guide for Native American Multimedia

Partners:_____   _____

Native American Research Project
by Lisa Allen

Name of Native American nation: _____

Name any reference books that you use. Write them down correctly. You must use at least three sources.

1._____

2._____

3._____

4._____

5._____

Card #1 Introduction Card—Give the name of the nation. Give the time period in history.

Card #2 Roles of Children and Adults—What kind of jobs did children have in the nation?

What kind of jobs did adults have in the nation?

Card #3 Individuals and Families—Then and Now—Describe how your life and your family's life is different from a child's life and a family's life in the nation?

How did they find food? Describe their food and your food.

Card #4 Beliefs and Practices—What were some beliefs and practices of the nation?

Card #5 Artistic Expression—What kind of artistic expression was found in the nation? (Examples: painting, music, dance, etc.)

Figure 3.11 Scoring Guidelines for Multimedia Project

NATIVE AMERICAN REPORT EVALUATION FORM
by Lisa Allen

Topic_____

Presenters_____

SOCIAL STUDIES CRITERIA
Research Component

1. The students presented information about the roles of children and adults in the tribe.

Poor			Fair			Good			Excellent	
0	1	2	3	4	5	6	7	8	9	10

2. The students presented information about the similarities and differences between their families' lives and the lives of the families in the tribe.

Poor			Fair			Good			Excellent	
0	1	2	3	4	5	6	7	8	9	10

3. The students presented information about the beliefs and practices of the tribe.

Poor			Fair			Good			Excellent	
0	1	2	3	4	5	6	7	8	9	10

4. The students presented information about artistic expression within the tribe.

Poor			Fair			Good			Excellent	
0	1	2	3	4	5	6	7	8	9	10

Hypermedia Component

1. The students have included a Title Card in their stack.

No	Yes
0	10

2. The stack has a minimum of 10 cards.

No										Yes
0	1	2	3	4	5	6	7	8	9	10

3. The stack includes scrolling and non-scrolling text fields.

No	Partially	Yes
0	5	10

4. The stack includes one (or more) geographic map.

No	Yes
0	10

5. The stack includes five (or more) pieces of clip art and background graphics.

No	Partially	Yes
0	5	10

6. The stack includes five (or more) pieces of original artwork.

No	Partially	Yes
0	5	10

7. The stack includes two (or more) sounds.

No	Partially	Yes
0	5	10

Planning at the unit level

The variety and flexibility of Mindful Learning strategies provides a rich resource for planning beyond the lesson level. Teachers in our graduate courses at UNC Greensboro have created a number of engaging "units" of study as they have explored Mindful Learning. Some last for several days; some for several weeks. One such unit is presented in the "Classroom Applications" at the end of this chapter. This unit, entitled "Owls and Ecosystems— Who gives a hoot?" presents a straightforward planning matrix organized by Gardner's (1983) seven frames of mind. Using this framework helps teachers see how many of the different ways of knowing they have tapped in their planning. It also helps them balance the modes of inquiry encouraged. This unit demonstrates a well-focused use of Mindful Learning strategies to help students grasp a core concept.

Conclusions

Lessons like the ones illustrated in this chapter put Mindful Learning into practice. These lessons begin with efforts to help students understand how they learn best. Whether they use paper-and-pencil activities, discussion-based approaches or specific mini-lessons, students learn the language of multiple intelligences. Teachers plan Mindful Learning lessons by incorporating strategies that emphasize different ways of knowing. For some concepts, using artifacts helps students make connections naturally. For other concepts, graphic organizers, decision charts, or cooperative learning groups may be more useful. Sometimes it is possible to offer students project options or to draw upon multimedia resources. No matter what form the lesson takes, students learn new concepts and new ways of knowing in an integrated fashion.

Classroom Applications
"An Interdisciplinary Unit for Sixth Grade"

Interdisciplinary Unit for Sixth Grade Developed by
Christine Baummer (Our Lady of Grace School)
Kelly McDuffie (Guilford County Schools)
and Karen Dixon (UNC Greensboro)

"OWLS AND ECOSYSTEMS — WHO GIVES A HOOT?"

GOAL STATEMENT: To help students be aware of the interactions between populations in ecosystems

OVERVIEW:	MATH	SCIENCE	LANG. ARTS	SOC. STUDIES
AREAS OF STUDY	graphing, problem-solving	interactions within eco-systems	poetry, communication skills	impact of humans on the environ-ment, individual differences
CONCEPTS	% problem solving strategies & data analysis	food web/ food chain; predator/prey	point of view, narrative writing, journaling	factors that produce change in environment
THINKING STRATEGIES	problem solving, application, interpretation	lab process, classification, application	role playing, interpretation, inference, critical thinking, application	processing background knowledge; application, mapping

INTRODUCTION TO THE UNIT: Our goal in this unit is to help students be aware of the interactions between populations in the environment. Throughout the week, we will try to help integrate across the disciplines a common theme of environments and ecosystems with a focus on owls. By the end of the week we hope to have made the students aware of themselves and touch on how they affect the environment.

We will begin the week with a visit from the raptor center. This will introduce students to owls and other birds of prey as well as pique their curiosity for this unit of study.

As a culminating activity, we have planned a trip to a local elementary school where the students will have the opportunity to share what they have learned about owls. Each student will make a plan on Thursday telling exactly what they will share at the elementary school. They may work in pairs or alone to present what they feel is interesting about owls.When we return to school, students will have reflection time and activities to help draw closure to our week-long study of owls.

SCHEDULE SUMMARY FOR THE WEEK: The Raptor Center will visit on Monday. The schedule will be changed to accommodate this. The team will take a trip to the elementary school on Friday morning. The afternoon will be spent in block time so that students are able to finish up their social studies journal activity and reflect on their morning at the elementary school.

SCIENCE:
Monday: introduction to food web and food chain,
            discuss relationship between predator and prey,
            ecosystem interactions
Tuesday: introduction to owls—anatomy of the digestive
            system, preliminary investigation of the owl pellets
Wednesday: begin dissection of owl pellets,
            separate bones, teeth, and fur
Thursday: sort and classify bones according to Bone Sorting
            Chart,
            create their own bone chart,
            glue bone skeletons onto paper and label
Friday: block time with social studies and language arts

MATH:
Monday: review metric measurement and weight to prepare
            students for Tuesday's science activity
Tuesday: review of graphing
Wednesday: game (adapted from Oh Deer!/Project Wild) to
            generate data about population interaction
Thursday: analyze and graph data from game and from owl
            pellet dissection in science
Friday: block time with social studies and language arts

SOCIAL STUDIES:
Monday: introduction to seven intelligences, assign week-
            long journal assignment

Tuesday: jigsaw to learn six types of owls native to NC and
            Europe
Wednesday: map owl habitats in regions of Europe,
            discuss of habitats of NC and where to find
            different types of owls
Thursday: watch video "Food for Pearl"
            discuss our impact on environment
Friday: block time to complete journal activity,
            discuss students' reactions to their own ways of
            learning

LANGUAGE ARTS:

Monday: write announcements to elementary school,
            make fold-up owl cards,
            prewriting/peer editing
Tuesday: read poetry related to owls
Wednesday: draft point-of-view narrative poem on owls
Thursday: complete planning sheet for elementary school
            visit,
            edit final draft of poem from Wednesday,
            evaluate writing process
Friday: block time to complete reflection activities

PHYSICAL EDUCATION: predator/prey games

MUSIC: Owl Hoots — identification of types of owls based
            on their call

ART   owl tessellations, chalk silhouettes

ADVISORY: make owl puppets for elementary school,
            introspective owl diaries,
            superstitions regarding owls

SCIENCE LESSON ILLUSTRATION: The focus of our science
class this week will be the investigation of owl pellets. After the
initial discussion on Monday about predator/prey relationships
and the effects of these relationships on the ecosystem, students
will begin to work in pairs with owl pellets. Before they actually
dissect the pellet, students must draw a picture of the pellet, mea-
sure and mass it, and write a paragraph describing it. Once this
process is complete, students will dissect their owl pellet. This re-

quires that they pull apart the pellet and separate the fur, bones, and teeth. By using the Bone Sorting Chart, they will sort and classify everything found. Tallies will be done of the amounts of each type of bone found, and this data will carry over to math class for analysis. In the final part of the dissection, students will "create" a skeleton (as complete as possible) from the bones found in the owl pellet. This skeleton will be glued onto paper and labeled. Once the bone data has been analyzed in math class, we can discuss in science class the results and what implications they have on the interactions of populations within the ecosystem.

MATH LESSON ILLUSTRATION: In math class this week, we will be reviewing concepts of measurements and graphing in order to relate data that the students collect. The review of measurements will prepare students for their science lesson on Tuesday where they investigate the owl pellets. On Wednesday, we will play a game in math class that will demonstrate what factors affect wildlife. The class will be divided into groups of equal size. One group (one-fourth of the class) will be the owls. The remaining students will choose to be either food, water, or shelter (components of their habitat). The owls will turn their backs and decide which "necessity" they want. This will be designated by a hand signal. They then search out that necessity from the other group of students (also designating themselves with hand signals). Every necessity captured by the owl becomes an owl, and every owl that could not get the chosen necessity dies and becomes a necessity. After every round, statistics are kept to show how the population varies. Then the hunter is introduced to show how humans can affect a population of owls. At the end of the game, all of the data is compiled and graphed to show how the population varies naturally and how human hunters can affect that.

SOCIAL STUDIES LESSON ILLUSTRATION: On Monday, all students on our team will be introduced to the seven intelligences as proposed by Gardner. After modeling the characteristics of each intelligence and clarifying discussion, students will be asked to make a prediction as to which intelligences will be their strengths and which will be their weaknesses. Throughout the unit, they will reflect on each lesson. Each teacher on the team allows three to four minutes at the end of class for students to record the following:

• describe the activity(ies) they completed within that class period,
• record their reactions,
• log that activity under the appropriate intelligence on a chart.

All students will turn in their journals and charts on Friday. This will be precipitated by a class discussion in which students see if their predictions as to their learning preferences were accurate or not and why; what they learned from this; which intelligences, if any, were emphasized by their teachers; and what could be done to improve instruction. The social studies teacher will use this as an assessment instrument.

LANGUAGE ARTS LESSON ILLUSTRATION: In preparation for our team visit to the local elementary school on Friday, students will write announcements to the students they will visit on the fold-up owl cards they have made on Monday. On Thursday, all students will complete a planning sheet on which they will record:

- what information from their owl unit they plan to share and why,
- what materials they will need to bring to present this,
- the name of their co-presenter (they can choose to present alone or with a friend),
- the job of each presenter

These will be turned in and kept until needed on Friday. After their visit, students will complete a reflection activity in which they record their thoughts on the back of Thursday's sheet. This reflection includes such questions as:

- What did you actually share and why?
- What were the reactions of the kids to whom you presented?
- What were your reactions?
- Would you do anything differently?
- What improvements would you recommend to the teacher?

These planning/reflection sheets will be collected and reviewed by the language arts teacher, who will then report to her team on student learning and lesson improvement.

UNIT SUMMARY — ACTIVITIES THAT REFLECT DIFFERENT TYPES OF LEARNING

Linguistic Activities	Mathematical Activities	Visual Activities	Kinesthetic Activities	Musical Activities	Interpersonal Activities	Intrapersonal Activities
telling story to elementary students	doing computations from the Oh Owl! game	drawing the food web	playing the Owl! game	creating Owl hoots		recording multiple intelligences journals

writing in journals	measuring	making the bone skeletons		Analyzing "The Eagle and The Hawk" song	making elementary school presentations	editing one's own work
writing announce-ments	graphing	watching "Food for Pearl" video	dissecting owl pellets / arrange bone skeletons		planning to visit the raptor center	reflecting on activities
reading poetry		making Owl tessellations	telling stories with puppets, making puppets and fold-up cards		working together in cooperative learning	making entries in the diaries
writing poetry		making chalk silhouettes of owl	playing predator /prey games in PE		peer editing of poetry	

RUBRIC ASSESSMENT:
POINT OF VIEW POEM IN LANGUAGE ARTS

This rubric is designed on a four-point scale. The team teachers decided that if a student turned in a poem, he or she would not receive a failing grade. Students will be allowed to rewrite their poems once if they are unhappy with the grade received. The comments made by the teacher will help them to see where their poem is lacking so they will know how to correct it.

$$4 = A$$
$$3 = B$$
$$2 = C$$
$$1 = D$$

To receive a 4:
- the poem is written with a clear point of view
- the poem incorporates creativity
- the poem demonstrates a clear understanding of interactions between owls and other populations in the ecosystem
- student uses correct mechanics (2 or fewer errors will be allowed)
- word choice enhances the overall quality of the poem

To receive a 3:

- the poem is written with a clear point of view
- the poem demonstrates a clear understanding of interactions between owls and other populations in the ecosystem
- student uses correct mechanics (3-4 errors will be allowed)
- word choice enhances the overall quality of the poem

To receive at 2:
- the point of view of the poem is vague but evident
- the poem demonstrates some understanding of interactions between owls and other populations in the ecosystem
- student uses somewhat correct mechanics (5-6 errors will be allowed)
- word choice does not enhance overall quality of the poem

To receive at 1:
- the point of view of the poem is vague or not evident
- the poem demonstrates little or no evidence of an understanding of interactions between owls and other populations in the ecosystem
- student has more than 6 mechanical errors
- word choice distracts from the unity and flow of the poem

RESEARCH ABSTRACTS

(summaries of two of the data-based studies referenced in this chapter as a resource for further reference and continued reading)

Garnett, K., & Bullock, J. (1991). Developing problem-solving heuristics in the middle school: A qualitative study. *Research in Middle Level Education,* *15* (1), 83–103.

Researchers analyzed the problem-solving responses of sixth graders who had daily practice with a structured, six-step strategy developed by Uprichard and Phillips (1982). The steps of this strategy are

1. Read to understand the problem statement.
2. Analyze the input to organize information and develop a plan.
3. Estimate a solution.
4. Translate the problem to mathematical language.
5. Compute to find a numerical solution.
6. Verify by comparing with estimate and checking computation.

The teacher observed students as they solved prepared problems and created and exchanged their own problems. Researchers then conducted structured interviews and analyzed problem-solving protocols. Data documented growth in problem solving in general and provided evidence for conclusions regarding successful instructional approaches: "systematic think aloud modeling, cooperative learning, frequent and diverse problem-solving experiences, consistent implementation of the model throughout the school year, journal writing, and guided questioning (p. 90).

Hawk, P. (1986). Graphic organizers: Increasing the achievement of life science students. *Middle School Research: Selected Studies 1986,* 16-23.

This study compared the performance of 390 sixth and seventh grade students who studied Life Science under two different conditions. Teachers gave the experimental group graphic organizers for each of the first seven chapters in their text. Students in the comparison group used the same textbook and completed the same activities without using graphic organizers. At the end of the semester, teachers administered a standardized unit test. Analysis of covariance showed that students who used the graphic organizers scored significantly higher on the unit test than did students in the comparison group, even when the prescores were used as a covariate.

CHAPTER-TO-CHAPTER CONNECTIONS

The preceding chapter presented a series of strategies for planning and teaching Mindful Learning lessons. This chapter extends those strategies to focus more specifically on teaching self-discipline. Three themes provide essential connections:

- For students to become less disruptive, they must first become more connected—connected with other people and with successful activities.
- Successful teachers work as teams of adults to support students as they think through their decisions about their behavior. These teachers establish long-range plans for supporting students in their efforts to learn self-discipline.
- Successful teachers encourage students to think through their choices and consequences in ways that build on their learning strengths and that provide both structure and support. Incorporating learning strengths into disciplinary interventions is a powerful dimension of Mindful Learning.

The chapter that follows features specific strategies for assessing progress toward self-discipline and academic achievement.

Chapter Four

Teaching Self-Discipline

> I want my teachers to think I am sweet. I am wild
> sometimes. I try to do good in my classes to get a good
> conduct grade on my report card. I might not be sweet
> anywhere else but I am sweet at school.
>
> "Mandy" in Strahan (1988, p. 384)

Mandy's comments to me in an interview years ago has come
back to me often as I visit classrooms. I see some students who try
very hard to get their classmates' attention, sometimes in ways
that strain the patience of their teachers. I see other students who
try not be noticed, to fade into whatever background the classroom can provide. Others, like Mandy, try to avoid trouble, even
when it tries to find them. With caring assistance from her teachers, Mandy learned to monitor her behavior and gained confidence in academic situations. She learned self-control.

Learning self-control is an essential dimension of Mindful Learning. As defined from the beginning of this text, Mindful Learning
begins with students' perceptions of themselves and school. Learning to identify choices and consequences is vital to both academic
and social success. Mindful Learning, at its best, integrates acade-
mics with positive discipline.

Teachers sometimes find it difficult to associate the words "positive" and "discipline." When I began teaching, I certainly did not
think of discipline as positive. Coming from a traditional teacher education program, I knew a great deal about my subject matter but
not nearly as much about students. I could design intricate units,
present well-planned lessons, and, occasionally, ask questions that
encouraged students to think. I viewed discipline as a "hassle," a
"necessary evil" of sorts that kept me from teaching. Fortunately, I
worked with some very patient young adolescents and some wise
colleagues who helped me learn that discipline can be positive. I
found ways to encourage students to develop respect and learn re-

sponsibility. Over time, I began to understand that positive discipline is self-discipline.

Now, more than twenty years later, I am convinced that helping students learn self-discipline is central to our mission as educators. My studies of students' perceptions of school (Strahan, 1988) and of successful approaches to self-discipline (Strahan, 1989) have underscored the importance of helping students see themselves as valuable, able, and responsible. Some students enter the middle grades believing that they cannot control themselves, convinced that other people cause them to say and do things they do not want to do or say. Some of these students are afraid that they will "lose control." Others are beginning to test their decision-making powers. Others are learning that they are responsible for their actions. Consequently, all students benefit from classroom practices that help them connect choices and consequences.

To help them do so, we must re-think some of our notions of "control." While the middle grades can be a time when students gain confidence in their abilities to think about their choices and control their own actions, it can also be a time when young adolescents and adults struggle over issues of control. The difference between positive discipline and negative discipline begins with ways that educators view the developmental needs of students and how they see themselves in the process. Arnold (1993) has described how young adolescents have often been the victims of negative stereotyping. One of the most powerful misperceptions is that "young adolescents are inherently id-driven, irrational, and argumentative" (p. 3). Educators who believe that students are likely to be "out of control" attempt to impose excessive structure. Inadvertently, they often create a "combat zone" mentality and schooling becomes a series of "us versus them" confrontations.

Positive discipline starts with a commitment to helping students learn self-discipline. Based on studies of successful approaches to classroom management (Purkey and Strahan, 1986; Strahan,1989; Colvin, Kameenui, & Sugai, 1993; Wang, Haertel, & Walberg, 1993)), this chapter offers suggestions for developmentally appropriate strategies for enhancing discipline. **The major premise of this chapter is that for students to become less disruptive, they must first become more connected.** "Connecting points" provide a basis for learning self-discipline (Strahan, 1989, p. 2). For example, some students misbehave more in some classes than others. Some students who work to be "kicked out" of English might not dream of missing math. Other students who act up to avoid going to music might never want to miss physical education. In the classes where they are learning self-control, they are "connected" with either the teacher or the subject matter. Understanding more about the dynamics of positive discipline may provide a basis for creating stronger connections with all students.

Understanding the reasons behind the actions

In earlier chapters, I have described some of the ways that young adolescents form concepts of themselves as individuals and establish identities in a negotiated fashion. A critical aspect of this identity formation is moral development, how young adolescents form notions of right and wrong. Teachers see these notions negotiated in classroom settings and are often most concerned about students who choose to be disruptive.

One of my studies of these dynamics (Strahan, 1988) has provided me a more specific understanding of ways students who see themselves as "troublemakers" play out their views of themselves and school. Using a matched group design, I compared writing samples and interview responses from a group of students who had "reconnected" in seventh grade with a similar group of students who had not done well and who were retained at the end of the year. Data documented ways that students who had been retained were "disconnected" from the academic world of their school. When describing their responses to lessons, they focused on "academic survival," getting help with assignments, looking busy, and staying out of trouble. Four of them noted specifically that they prided themselves in creating disruptions. They made specific references to fighting with other students and "getting into it" with teachers.

Students in the comparison group, in contrast, frequently expressed perceptions of themselves as "making progress" and "doing better than last year." Successful students reported functional strategies for completing assignments. Like Mandy's comment at the beginning of this chapter, many of them suggested that

they tried to avoid getting in trouble. Students who entered seventh grade with negative attitudes toward school and found ways to get better grades and control their behavior attributed their successes to specific teachers and specific projects. They talked about the teachers who spent time with them and the projects and assignments they completed successfully. The study concluded that

> Positive school experiences for students in the marginal group were connected with specific teachers or types of activities. The constructive views of themselves that they expressed on occasion were associated with specific reinforcement of good grades on particular assignments, with special activities and games or with special events such as the planting of trees in a school beautification project. (p. 386)

Based on this study and my experiences in working with disruptive students since that time, I am convinced that the dynamics of positive discipline are interactive. Students who are disruptive usually feel disconnected from the academic world of school. To begin to think through their choices and the consequences of their actions, they need to establish working relationships with teachers and peers. They may be skeptical of adults in authority. They may resent the school success of other students. They may feel dissociated from the academic conversations of the classroom. Whatever their past experiences, learning to be successful at school begins with the people in the process (Purkey and Strahan, 1986).

How can teachers encourage success and self-control?

Teachers who wish to encourage success and self-control must find ways to develop working relationships and provide ongoing success. To do so, teachers must understand that their own actions are guided by the same dynamics that guide students' actions: the pictures they carry in their heads of themselves and their students (Glasser, 1986). Studies of teachers' thought processes have described a number of ways that instructional decisions are based on deep-seated "orientations" toward teaching and learning (Strahan, 1989). How teachers view themselves, their subject matter, and the processes of teaching determine the ways they view classroom events and the ways they make instructional decisions. Teachers' views of individual students play a critical role in these interactions. When they view certain students as "unable" or "irresponsible," they treat them accordingly.

Researchers have documented ways that these "expectations" shape behavior (Good & Weinstein, 1986; Colvin, Kameenui, & Sugai, 1993)). For both teachers and students, "creating connections" and minimizing disruptions requires the formation of new pictures, pictures based on successful images of what students can do rather than on recollections of what they cannot do. Such pictures are formed by messages as well as experiences.

In *Positive Discipline: A Pocketful of Ideas* (Purkey and Strahan, 1986) William Purkey and I explore the essential role of "messages" in inviting self-discipline. Our review of the literature on successful teaching emphasizes the importance of "the person in the process" and the messages that a person sends and receives. When working with disconnected and disruptive students, three messages are especially critical:

> **"YOU ARE VALUABLE."** To succeed in school, students need to feel that they belong, that others cares about them,

and that they can care for others. Working relationships begin with personal relationships. Helping students see themselves as valuable is the first step in helping them think through choices and consequences.

"YOU ARE ABLE." Students who see themselves as troublemakers may believe that they are unable to control their behavior. Practice in verbalizing the choices they make encourages confidence. Learning that they are able to connect choices and consequences is a second key step.

"YOU ARE RESPONSIBLE." Accepting responsibility for the consequences of choices is the essence of self-discipline. Some students believe that other people and outside events control one's actions. Unlearning that belief is the third critical aspect of self-discipline.

Mindful Learning encourages students to process these messages in a connected way. Knowing that they matter to someone, that they can make successful decisions, and that teachers care enough to hold them accountable provides a foundation for learning more about self-discipline.

One of the most important aspects of preparation is defining our expectations for positive discipline. Stating our expectations clearly encourages self-discipline. A number of teams have developed memorable frameworks for stating their expectations. One of the most effective statements focuses on the theme of respect:

> Respect yourself and the rest of us.
> Enjoy our time together.
> See the value of everyone.
> Pay attention to the person speaking.
> Encourage your classmates.
> Commit to do your very best.
> Take responsibility for your choices.

A framework like this can set the stage for a series of discussions about behavior. Students can help us clarify our expectations and encourage a sense of community. They can suggest interesting ways to build on the concept of respect—perhaps even find a song or two to use as "themes." By preparing for positive discipline, we establish a climate that makes it possible to be more supportive when disruptions occur.

Positive Disciplinary Processes

In *Positive Discipline: A Pocketful of Ideas*, we describe a model for encouraging self-discipline and cooperation in the classroom. Our studies of teachers who are most successful with classroom management demonstrate ways that positive discipline proceeds in three stages. In the first stage, preparation, teachers anticipate students' needs for supportive interventions and strive to prevent disruptions. In the second stage, teachers "respond" to disruptions when they occur by employing systematic strategies in a caring fashion. In the final stage, or "follow-up," teachers attempt to develop trusting relationships with students over time. Basic to success in all of these phases are the beliefs that students can learn self-control, that teaching self-control is one of the most important responsibilities of a teacher, and that connecting choices and consequences provides a vehicle for learning self-control.

The preparation stage. Purkey and Strahan (1986) suggest that positive discipline begins with teachers' attitudes toward their students. Successful teachers want discipline to be positive and believe that most of their students want to behave most of the time. This attitude of "expecting good things" becomes especially important in sending supportive messages through discipline. In his studies of successful classroom managers, Brophy (1983) found that the "seemingly automatic" routines of successful teachers result from careful preparation.

> This study made it clear that the seemingly automatic, smooth-functioning routines observable in the classrooms of successful managers result from a great deal of preparation and organization at the beginning of the year. (p. 269)

Successful teachers consistently demonstrate two essential characteristics of effective management: they anticipate decisions and view discipline as "teaching" rather than control. Brophy found studies of successful interventions seemed to "implicitly agree on a set of common principles" which included respect for individual differences, willingness to work with students individually, emphasis on teaching, and persuasion rather than power (p. 282). He concluded that

> these approaches also recognize that students have responsibilities along with their rights, and that they will have to suf-

fer the consequences if they persist in failing to fulfill those responsibilities. (p. 282)

These expectations are especially important as teachers respond to individual students. Most teachers have one or two students that they view as especially "challenging." Creating more positive connections with these students begins with an awareness of our attitudes toward them. Successful interventions begin the realization that our own attitudes shape our behaviors. If we become aware that we have a tendency to "rejoice" when one of our students is absent, we can begin to find ways to generate more positive perceptions of that student. Until we do so, we are likely to keep playing out self-fulfilling prophecies.

These attitudes set the stage for careful planning and preparation. Preventive discipline depends on planning lessons that are engaging and organizing time and space in ways that encourage students to stay on task. Knowledge of developmental differences is absolutely essential to the anticipation and prevention of disruptions.

A developmental perspective is most important in reading situations. Before they respond to a potential disruption, successful teachers take a few seconds to try to figure out just what is occurring and decide what messages they want to send. The way a teacher interprets an event will determine much of what follows. For example, if a teacher thinks that a student is trying to impress his friends by being clever, she might be inclined to play down a "class clown" type disruption. She might use humor to give him a bit of recognition. If she sees his behavior as an act of defiance and a threat to her authority, she might inadvertently escalate the situation. The confrontation could result in a shouting match with major repercussions. In almost every instance, how teachers read situations determines their responses. As difficult as it may be in the pressure of the moment, successful teachers remember that each disruption is a teaching incident and try to proceed accordingly.

The initiating/responding stage. Purkey and Strahan (1986) describe a number of ways that successful teachers make disciplinary decisions based on what they know about individual students. Based on their reading of situations, they act in ways that are most likely to redirect students back to academic tasks and encourage engagement among other students as well. The following situation demonstrates a familiar scenario:

> Students in a particular seventh grade class are working on group projects. The teacher is seated with one group and is talking with them about ways to gather additional information. In the far corner of the room, a student gets out of her seat and goes over to talk with a friend in another group. Without leaving her group, the teacher signals with her hands. The girl reluctantly walks to the teachers' group and waits until the teacher stops to talk with her.

Scenes such as this occur hundreds of times each day in middle-level classrooms. The teacher in this scene is sending many messages simultaneously:

> I see you.
> It's not OK to go talk with your friend right now.
> What I'm doing with this group is important.
> You are important, too.
> We are going to keep working as best we can.
> Please wait until I reach a good stopping point.
> Let's talk about what you need right now.

In this scene, the individual is reassured that her needs matter and the rest of the class is reminded that the work matters, too. Purkey and Strahan (1986) suggest that successful teachers send many messages as they respond to classroom disruptions. As a strategy of organizing these messages in a meaningful way, they suggest that teachers "play their low cards first" (p. 20). They note that beginning with unobtrusive "low cards" gives teachers a chance to address disruptions without breaking the flow of lessons or interrupting students who are on-task. Playing "high cards" too soon may turn a small incident into a power play and escalate the problem (p. 19). As an illustration, they describe the following low card/high card sequence employed by a teacher who notices that two students are talking while he gives directions:

> raising eyebrows in an inquisitive fashion
> staring politely (steady gaze)
> pausing briefly while continuing to stare
> moving closer to the students while continuing to talk
> gently placing a hand on one of the student's shoulders while continuing to give directions
> using a student's name as part of the lesson ("Mary, what would be a good due date ?)"
> asking the student by name to listen to directions
> asking the student, "What did I ask you to do?"
> asking the student to meet after class
> asking the student to move to a "time out" area in the room
> assigning penalties. (p. 19–20)

Over time, successful teachers develop extensive repertoires of "low cards." They learn to play certain cards with certain individuals and save their "high cards" for cases in which they are needed.

Not only do teachers need to send a variety of messages, they need to be sure that messages are received. As Purkey and Strahan (1986) indicate, this notion of "insuring reception" is another key to successful discipline. By moving closer to students, observing their responses, talking with them briefly in class or more extensively after class, teachers can make sure that students understand what is expected and can decide how they wish to respond. These efforts can help maintain the communication flow of the classroom (p. 20).

The follow-up stage. In their interactions with students, successful teachers have learned that one of the keys to learning self-discipline is what happens after the disruption (Ringer, Doerr, Hollenshead, & Wills, 1993). Helping students connect their choices and consequences requires "processing," opportunities to think about their actions and their effects, to replay events, and to gain confidence in making better choices. For some students, connections between choices and consequences are so remote that this processing needs to be intensive. Purkey and Strahan (1986) suggest that the follow-up stage includes four related dimensions: interpreting responses, negotiating, evaluating outcomes, and developing trust. Once a disruption has been addressed, successful teachers watch and listen carefully to interpret student responses. Sometimes students readily accept their consequences and appear eager to resume classroom activities. Sometimes they appear angry or hostile. Successful teachers know that students may need to mask their responses. Whatever their response, what happens the day after a big confrontation is very important. Many of us can remember instances from our childhoods when we "got into trouble." Sometimes we can remember being angry at a parent and blaming them for the trouble. Sometimes we can also remember finding out why what we did was wrong and, equally importantly, learning that even though we made a mistake, our parent still loved us. Instances like that are very important. They help us learn about our choices and their consequences. They also help us learn to sort out our actions and our evaluations of ourselves as people.

Successful teachers know that students in the middle grades often have a very fragile sense of self-esteem. Acting tough, pretending not to care, or appearing indifferent may be ways of maintaining a sense of pride. Students who act up and act out may sometimes fall victim to a self-fulfilling prophecy. They do not believe they can control their own behavior. They expect other people to get frustrated with them. Their frustration fuels a sense of alienation that leads to further disruption. After a confrontation with a teacher, a student may find himself thinking, "I knew he didn't like me. This just proves it. I'll show him." Successful teachers have learned that the first step in developing working relationships is not buying in to these cycles of failure. Working things out after a disruption becomes an opportunity to develop trust. Successful teachers are committed to helping students learn that while their actions may not always be acceptable, they *are* accepted as people.

To establish better working relationships, teachers need to constantly evaluate the outcomes of their efforts. Successful teachers remember that their students have developed patterns of behavior over at least a ten-year period and that those patterns are not going to change instantly. They have learned to watch for progress over time and to focus on weeks and months rather than on hours and days. They have also learned that the true goal of discipline is self-discipline, not teacher control.

Some actions may have short-term impact in establishing teacher control at the expense of long-term detriment. The familiar practices of having students write sentences as punishment, do extra homework, or take quizzes as a consequence for misbehavior illustrate these dynamics. Writing sentences as punishment creates feelings of resentment toward both the teacher and the act of writing. Extra homework equates out-of-class assignments as punishment and suggests that school work is to be avoided. Giving quizzes has the same effect. In evaluating the effects of their disciplinary actions, teachers need to ask not only "Is this working?" but also "What messages am I sending?"

Positive discipline processes are attempts to create classroom climates in which students gain confidence in their abilities to make good choices and develop trust toward each other and the teacher. In classrooms where teachers and students can talk with others about their feelings and their decisions in a supportive fashion, it seems inevitable that discipline will be positive. Studies have shown that when teachers work together in a school-wide effort to approach discipline systematically, efforts are even more successful (Gottfredson, Gottfredson, and Hybl, 1993).

Positive discipline with individual students

Teachers who have learned to put these ideas into practice send powerful messages to their students. They provide support along

with structure. Moreover, they affirm students' ownership of their behavior. In essence, they are saying, "I care enough about you to hold you responsible." This type of caring readily translates into action.

My experience suggests that a positive discipline approach addresses most of the disruptions in a classroom most of the time. Some types of disruptions are more severe, however, and some students need much more intensive intervention. In working with students who are frequently disruptive, I have found Glasser's "Reality Therapy" approach adds another dimension of caring in action.

Beginning with a basic framework

Glasser's approach suggests that the key to self-control is learning to connect "choices" and "consequences" in a natural fashion. As first defined in "A new look at discipline," Glasser (1974) advocates a ten-step procedure for working with students who are frequently disruptive. When students misbehave, Glasser suggests that teachers take as many of the steps, in order, as may be necessary to solve the problem or reach an agreement. The gist of these ten steps are as follows:

1. List what you are doing with the student now that is not working.
2. Try to give the student a fresh start.
3. Find at least one thing to do for the student that can help him or her have a better day tomorrow.
4. Offer corrective solutions in a calm, quiet manner and give the student a chance to accept the correction.
5. Ask the student to make a plan to follow the rules.
6. Schedule a conference. This gives the teacher a chance to listen to the student, get to know the student better, and try to work out a plan to follow the rules.
7. Assign "time out" in the room. Separate the student from the rest of class in a comfortable place that is close enough to hear the lesson. The student can return to the rest of the class when he or she has a plan for controlling behavior.
8. Assign time out at the office. An administrator should talk with the student to reinforce the need to make, and keep, a plan.
9. Put the student on a "tolerance day" contract specifying that the student comes to school in the morning and stays as long as he or she honors the plan. If he or she misbehaves, the parents must come and take the student home.
10. Remove the student from school. (paraphrased from pp. 6–11).

This procedure, based on Glasser's successful interventions with juvenile delinquents, has provided the basis for a number of effective behavioral therapy programs since its first publication. In the first three steps, Glasser encourages teachers to carefully examine what they are currently doing by retracing their actions to date, planning new interventions, and trying to improve their relationships with challenging students. The next three steps implement a "nonpunitive" approach in which students are asked to stop disruptive behaviors, are required to generate their own plans for corrective action, and are given support for developing their plans through individual conferences. The final steps are a "graduated series of benching techniques" (p. 9). If disruptions continue, students are assigned to "time-out" spaces within the room and are asked to come up with an improved plan. If disruptions continue, students are assigned to supervised "time-out" spaces outside the classroom and, if absolutely necessary, assigned to a "tolerance day" system in which a parent must come to school and get them if they lose control. During the final step of the plan, teachers and administrators work with community agencies to try to help students change their behaviors (p. 11).

Over the past twenty years, many teachers and schools have employed Glasser's approach with great success. Medick (1981) presents one of the most detailed descriptions of Glasser's approach in action. Her case studies demonstrate ways that students learned to connect their choices and consequences over time. Working with parents and administrators, Medick encouraged students to feel better about themselves and to assume responsibility for their own actions. By refusing to buy into students hostile-aggressive or passive-aggressive behaviors, Medick demonstrated that it is possible for caring teachers and administrators to develop therapeutic interventions for individual students. In her conclusions, she emphasized the personal nature of the interactions that proved successful.

> Change occurs when a person owns his own problems, assumes responsibility for his own behavior, and wants to change. The strategies offered in this book allow no game-playing. Disruptive children are put in a choice-making position, kindly but firmly: follow reasonable rules or be removed from classroom activities. Disruption is stopped quickly, in a fair and non-punitive way. The teacher need not become upset or angry. He/she is free to teach, students are free to learn, and predominantly good feelings are experienced by all. (pp. 145–146)

As Medick has indicated, it takes time and teamwork to put Glasser's approach into practice. As tempting as it may be to want to "fix" discipline problems quickly, we must remember that we are often dealing with deeply ingrained patterns of behavior. Helping students learn to connect choices and consequences may require learning a new set of mental habits. Over time, the process can be-

---

Figure 4.1 Encouraging Self-Discipline: Questions to Guide Team Planning

WHAT IS HAPPENING WITH _____?
1. What is _____ doing?
2. Why might _____ be making the choices he or she is making?
3. How does _____ learn best?
   through art?   logic?   talking/listening/reading?
   music?   movement?   group work?   independent work?

WHAT ARE WE CURRENTLY DOING WITH _____?
4. How are we responding to _____'s behaviors?
5. What messages are we sending?
6. How can we help _____ connect choices and consequences?
   through art?   logic?   talking/listening/reading?
   music?   movement?   group work?   independent work?

HOW CAN WE ENCOURAGE POSITIVE DISCIPLINE?
7. Who can we enlist to help us work with _____?
   a. Who are the significant people in his or her life that can help?
   b. What resources are available to us?
8. How can we work together to develop plans of action?

---

come proactive. For example, Larson (1992) found that programs that focus on anger management and problem solving may be valuable in preventative efforts as well as in interventions.

Mindful Learning can provide a vehicle for linking supportive interventions with teamwork. Figure 4.1 presents a set of guiding questions for teams to use to develop more successful strategies for helping individual students connect choices and consequences. These questions link the basic steps of Reality Therapy with the "think about thinking" approach of Mindful Learning.

I have seen this approach work very successfully with many students over the years. Again, the keys seem to be the messages sent to the student:

> We care about and want you to be a successful member of this class.
> We believe you can control your actions.
> We will help you develop a plan.
> We will hold you responsible for your choices and their consequences.
> We will not give up on you or let you give up on yourself.

As indicated in *Control theory in the classroom* (1986), teachers and administrators who have been most successful with this approach have learned that positive discipline begins with their own attitudes and is based on their personal interactions with students. They have accepted the fact that since negative patterns have developed over years, positive patterns will develop slowly and that patience is the essence of the process. In most cases, they have formed teams of fellow teachers and administrators to support their efforts and have found ways to involve parents in the process. They have learned that positive discipline takes careful preparation as well as a commitment to look beyond behaviors to the reasons for actions and to work with students in a trusting fashion. In response to their efforts, they have observed students develop more self-control and gain confidence in their abilities to make wise decisions.

Teaching respect and responsibility through Mindful Learning

Mindful Learning suggests a powerful set of principles that can help students learn self-control even more explicitly. As suggested throughout the text, students learn best when affective and academic concepts are integrated. Most of the classroom illustrations have connected affective concepts such as self-esteem and caring for others with academic concepts in language arts, math, science, and socials studies. Using what we have learned about teaching affective and academic concepts, we have recently begun to develop strategies for teaching respect and responsibility more specifically.

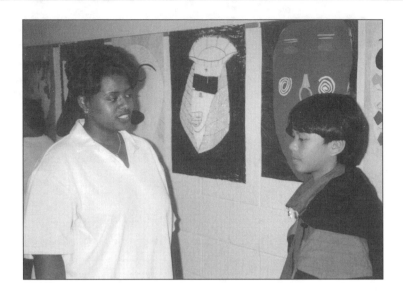

The following strategies provide a range of options for tapping students' individual ways of learning:

Logical learning

Students who approach ideas in a logical fashion can readily connect choices and consequences in an "if __, then __" fashion. Strategies for tapping this talent include sequence charts that map events in terms of decisions and outcomes, time lines that chronicle choices and consequences, and hypothetical scenarios in which students can chart alternatives for conflict resolution. Students who learn logically may benefit from interventions that feature very specific individual contracts.

Artistic learning

Students who process information visually can often link decisions and outcomes through pictorial representations. Strategies for tapping this talent include showing video clips in which characters make decisions, illustrated flow charts of events, and comic strip scenarios that can be completed in different ways. Students who learn visually may benefit from interventions that help them structure their alternative pathways for avoiding conflict or disruption.

Linguistic learning

Students who learn best through talking, listening, reading, and writing can often connect choices and consequences through stories and discussion. A powerful strategy for tapping this talent is bibliotherapy. By selecting stories in which characters face similar situations, teachers can provide an opportunity to think through choices and consequences with structure. Analyzing the characters' options is a non-threatening way to introduce ideas that students can apply to their own situations. Students who learn verbally may benefit from interventions that require them to talk through "if __, then __" possibilities in conference fashion and make commitments accordingly.

Musical learning

Students who approach ideas through sound and rhythm can often benefit from analyzing situations through songs and lyrics. Asking them to create their own musical collages that illustrate a range of situations and options for resolution can be very effective. "Best" options can then be incorporated into individual contracts.

Moving to learn

Students who learn best through movement may find it helpful to participate in role playing situations in which they can walk through scenarios and then think through choices and consequences. One especially productive intervention is "walking advisement." It is often much easier for some students to talk about their situations with a teacher or peer helper while walking through the school or on the grounds. Ideas mapped out "on the walk" can then be structured into written agreements.

Interpersonal learning.

Students who process information through social interactions can often analyze decisions and outcomes through small group meetings and one-to-one conversations. Strategies for tapping this talent include group projects and mentoring. Students who learn socially may benefit from interventions that involve a "significant other person," a relative, coach, or older friend who can offer guidance and support as well monitor expectations.

Intrapersonal learning

This same approach can also benefit students who process information in a more introspective fashion. Asking students to keep a journal in which they record events and feelings may be a good way to tap their talent for reflection. Students who learn intrapersonally may often be able to generate their own solutions which can be supported and monitored by a mentor.

Teaching self-discipline—An illustration

The case study that follows provides an illustration of some of the ways a Mindful Learning approach might help a teacher and his team mates develop strategies for more positive discipline with one of their students. The first portion of this case study is the report that a teacher prepared to share with his team regarding his interactions with "Stan." Following this report is the log of the team meeting outlining a plan of action.

Case Study — Stan

9/2 OBSERVATIONS: Stan arrived [late] to our orientation session for Reading Lab, announced to everyone that he had been to the counselor's office, "trying to get out of this dummy class." When I asked him to take a seat, he threw his books on the desk and they fell to the floor. I picked them up for him and waited until he sat down. During the rest of the meeting, he made "angry" faces at other students and remained quiet. At dismissal, he bolted out of the room.

REFLECTIONS: I had met Stan briefly during our scheduling meeting. He did not seem interested in the Reading Lab but I did not pick up any anger either. His outburst in this session surprised me. We scheduled him into lab because he had a low score on his End-of-Grade Reading Test in fifth grade and his teacher recommended him. I need to see Mrs. Smith (counselor) to see what is going on. Mrs. Smith reported that Stan told her he was in the elementary reading lab last year and "hated it." She suggested that this was a different school and that Stan would like the lab. It may take us a while to convince him of that.

9/3 OBSERVATIONS: The first regular day for lab—As I greeted students at the door, I asked Stan if we could talk later. We began class with a discussion of different ways people use reading and started planning our "real world reading" project. [Students are to investigate a type of work that interests them and list ways that reading and writing are used.] Once students settled in to their first journal entry ("When I'm 24—what I hope to be doing"), I asked Stan to talk with me at my desk. I asked him what was troubling him about the lab. He said "everyone knows this is a dummy class. I hate these things. I know how to read." I told him that Reading Lab was designed to break the stereotype of a "dummy class" and he was scheduled into the lab because his elementary teachers had recommended him. I told him that I would give him a chance to show what he could do.

REFLECTIONS: Stan's nonverbals are hard to read. He still seems angry but I am not sure why. He does not seem to want to talk to me about it and is still quietly hostile. Maybe he will open up a bit more during group work.

9/4 OBSERVATIONS: Today we continued to plan our "real world reading" projects. Almost all of the students shared their career goals from their journal entries yesterday. Several suggested ways that reading and writing are important and ways that study strategies related to the "real" world. After the first 15 minutes, Stan had not said anything so I called on him. He replied (sarcastically)

"Everyone knows that you have to read to get a job. This is stupid." I noticed that the other students seemed put off by his response. I decided to let it go and we went on to list other applications. When I asked students to work with partners to draft plans for their "real world reading" project, I noticed that no one wanted to work with Stan. I asked Rob to work with him. Rob turned in good notes indicating that he was going to investigate "video game design" and listing several people he would interview. For Stan, he listed "mechanic???" and told me "Stan didn't say much."

REFLECTIONS: Stan does not seem to be making much of an effort to work with his classmates. I thought he would get along with Rob. The next step seems to be to learn more about his reading.

9/5 OBSERVATIONS: I began my individual reading assessments today (using the *Qualitative Reading Inventory*). I gave students an option to read a book of their choice or to go to the media center while I met with individuals to give the QRI. Rob volunteered to go first. Stan stared out the window while I met with Rob so I called on him next. Stan said "I have taken these dumb tests before. Do I have to do this again?" I explained [again] that this was my way of learning how well students read and what they might do better. I began with a fourth grade passage. Stan struggled with word recognition (22 miscues in 200 words). When he came to words he did not know, he guessed quickly or skipped them. He answered four of the six comprehension questions correctly. He did best on the inferential questions. I asked him to read the fifth grade passage silently and he answered 2 of the questions correctly — again the inferential questions. When he was finished, he asked me "Did I read well enough to get out of here?" I explained to him that his comprehension was strong and that the lab could help him with word recognition. He replied "Well, does that mean I can get out of here?" I told him I would schedule a conference with Mrs. Smith next week to discuss the situation.

REFLECTIONS: Stan seems to be able to think through comprehension questions fairly well, especially since he struggles with word recognition. I noticed that he had very few functional strategies for sounding out words and very little patience with his reading. He seemed anxious to read quickly and get it over with. While his answers to inferential questions were on the mark, he was reluctant to elaborate his insights, answering my questions with two or three word responses.

9/6 OBSERVATIONS: Since it was Friday, I decided to do something a bit different. Each year, I like to teach students to play chess. [I think it encourages logic and some students seem to get into it.] Stan did very well. He said that his older brother taught him how to play and he knew most of the moves. When Cathy asked me to explain the moves again, he muttered, "What a dummy" loud enough for me to hear it. I asked him to "cool it" and he made an angry face. He won his first game quickly and poked fun at his partner (Rob). I asked him to show Rob some of his strategy and he explained a bit about protecting pieces (reluctantly).

REFLECTIONS: Here again, Stan showed talent for logic. I am still concerned about his attitude. He is beginning to put down his classmates. Next week we will need to decide whether he stays in lab or not. I am going to ask the team to meet on Wed.

9/9 Stan was absent.

9/10 OBSERVATIONS: Stan asked if we could play chess again. I explained that we would have some game time Friday and that I would be willing to play him then. I asked him to select a book to read or to go to the media center. He spent most of the class "browsing" through the book cases. At the end of class, when Cathy was returning to her desk after her QRI, Stan hit her chair with his foot, causing her to fall. As I walked over, she called him a name. He looked at me and said, "It was an accident." I asked him to discuss this with me later.

REFLECTIONS: I am not sure what to do next. Stan seemed puzzled when I offered to play chess with him on Friday—like he was not sure about playing the teacher (or whether it was worth staying in lab??) I really do not think he hit Cathy's chair accidently. I am glad we are having this team meeting tomorrow.

TEAM MEETING, 9/11- first period, Ms. J., recorder

Our first topic for discussion was Mr. B's request to address his concerns about Stan's behavior. He shared his notes with us and opened the meeting for discussion. He asked the rest of us to describe how Stan was doing in our classes.

- Ms. M. reported that Stan was not doing well in social studies (had turned in only two homework papers, never volunteered in class, had failed the first quiz).
- Ms. S. noted that his work in language arts was about the same (no homework grades, little participation, zero on his first quiz).
- Mr. L. said he was surprised to hear Stan was having difficulty in other classes and reported that his work in math was pretty good (80% on homework, some participation, 95% on quizzes).
- I noted that his work in science was mixed (90% on labs, 60% on quizzes, good participation in labs, not much response in discussion).

Mr. B. then asked about Stan's behavior:

- In social studies, Ms. M. noted that he said little, seemed sullen, did not draw much attention to himself.
- His behavior in language arts was very similar except that he sometimes made fun of other students having difficulty, especially when they read aloud, something he refused to do. Ms. S. reported that she, too, had tried to talk with Stan without much response.
- Mr. L. reported that Stan was usually pretty cooperative, especially when he could work with Mike and Alan. "I think they are a good influence on him."
- I noted that he often worked with them on his labs in science, and showed a tendency to take the lead when writing up the experiments.

Mr. B. asked for suggestions. Our ideas were as follows:

- Try to use his strengths in math and science to build success in reading.
- Tap his strengths with logic to evaluate the data from his reading assessments, ask him to help with a plan for improvement.

- If that does not help, Mr. L. and I will conference with Mr. B. to try to help Stan understand his reading needs and come up with a plan
- Encourage his interest in chess as a way to improve his relationship with Mr. B.

Mr. B. will report back in two weeks.

In this illustration, Stan's teachers are working as a team to understand him better and find ways to encourage positive discipline. They are applying the concepts of Mindful Learning to try to identify his learning strengths and tap those strengths to help him learn more about himself. Over time, they may be able to help him learn to read better, feel better about himself as a student, and control his behavior more successfully.

Conclusions

In this chapter, I have suggested that efforts to improve behavior begin with a commitment to helping students learn self-discipline. To do so, we may need to re-think our notions of "control." When we encourage self-control by sharing control, schools become less like "combat zones" and more like the "teaching zones" we wish for ourselves and our students. When we understand more about developmental differences, we are more likely to see why students sometimes misbehave. We can then proceed with careful examination of our own actions and respond in more developmentally appropriate ways. With our most challenging students, we can work as teams of adults to support students as they think through their decisions about their behavior. We can establish long-range plans for supporting students in their efforts to learn self-discipline. Through this type of caring in action, teachers are able to combine support and structure in providing positive discipline.

Encouraging students to think through their choices and consequences in ways that build on their learning strengths provides both structure and support. This approach fosters respect by beginning with sensitivity to individual differences and a willingness to work on an individual basis. This approach also fosters responsibility by expecting students to generate their own solutions and to evaluate their actions accordingly. Incorporating learning strengths into disciplinary interventions is thus a powerful dimension of Mindful Learning. Students can see that their ways of knowing can help them learn life skills as well as academic concepts.

Classroom Applications

"Flow Charting Choices about Fighting"

The chart on the opposite page shows one way that a student might chart choices and consequences related to fighting.

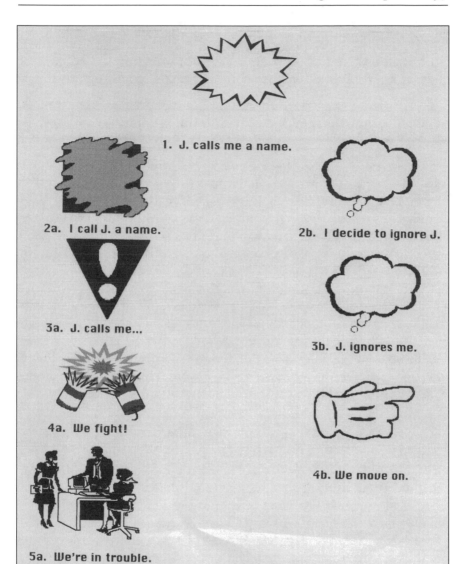

RESEARCH ABSTRACTS

(summaries of two of the data-based studies referenced in this chapter as a resource for further reference and continued reading)

Gottfredson, D., Gottfredson, G., and Hybl, L. (1993). Managing adolescent behavior: A multiyear, multischool study. *American Educational Research Journal*, 30 (1), 179–215.

Data from 5,719 students at eight middle schools provided a basis for analyzing programmatic aspects of school discipline. Six of the schools were implementing a schoolwide program featuring review/revision of discipline policies, behavior tracking systems, classroom management strategies, and positive reinforcement. The other two schools served as controls. Five different types of data were collected: classroom environment surveys, teacher ratings of disruption, student questionnaires, teacher survey of implementation, and school discipline records. Results showed that effects differed by level of implementation. Students in schools with high levels of implementation reported less punishment. Teachers reported higher perceptions of orderliness. Researchers concluded that discipline in middle schools can be improved and that administrative support is the key to implementation.

Larson, J. (1992). Anger and aggression management techniques through the Think First Curriculum. *Journal of Offender Rehabilitation*, 18 (1/2), 101-117. Forty-eight students from a large urban middle school who had been assigned to a program for children at risk participated in two different types of interventions. One group was randomly assigned to participate in the "Think First Program" in which they learned a self-instructional procedure for anger-aggression control through ten sessions of modelling and role playing. The control group participated in more traditional discussions. Results showed a significant decline in discipline referrals among students in the experimental group and offer modest support for the program. The author concludes that programs that focus on anger management and problem solving may be valuable in preventive efforts as well as in interventions.

CHAPTER-TO-CHAPTER CONNECTIONS

The first two chapters in this section presented strategies for developing Mindful Learning lessons and promoting a Mindful Learning approach to positive discipline. This chapter describes strategies for assessing students' progress toward academic achievement and self-discipline. Four basic principles connect Mindful assessment practices:

- Assessment should involve students. Learning to assess their own understanding and to monitor their own progress is essential to academic success and self-discipline.

- Forms of assessment should reflect purposes. Assessment toward understanding content should focus on essential academic concepts. Assessment toward proficiency should focus on learning strategies.

- Assessment should be ongoing. Instructional activities provide opportunities for teachers to assess understanding and progress on a continuous basis.

- Assessment decisions should reflect as many data sources as possible. Grades should represent a series of performances, not just a single test. Teachers can record observations, review assignments and confer with students.

This chapter presents specific strategies for putting these principles into practice. The chapter that follows offers suggestions for promoting Mindful Learning through teamwork and school-wide efforts.

Chapter Five

Assessing Progress

> Today's classroom observations were some of the most vivid yet. The teacher asked students to create "wanted posters" for the characters in *Number the Stars*. We noted that Daniel's level of involvement was much higher than had been the case in last week's lesson. At each of my recording intervals, he was drawing intently. Ellen's involvement was about as it had been. She drew for while, stopped, drew some more. At the end of the lesson, we asked to see their posters. Daniel brought us a very intricate drawing of a young girl with dark hair and delicate features. Ellen's drawing was less detailed. When we asked them to tell us about the activity, Daniel noted he liked to draw. Ellen described how the poster fit the character Anne Marie. When we asked the purpose of the activity, Daniel said, "I guess it will help me if I want to be an artist." Ellen said, "I think the teacher wants us to create a picture of Anne Marie so we can get more of her feelings."
>
> D. Strahan, Researcher's log, 4/20/95

If I had been required to "grade" the drawings that Daniel and Ellen showed me without the benefit of conversation, I am sure I would given Daniel an "A+" and probably would have given Ellen a "B." I would have assumed that Daniel had created a detailed visual representation of Anne Marie and that Ellen's picture was a bit vague. Once I talked with them, I revised my thinking. Ellen expressed very perceptive connections between the activity and the novel. Daniel had a hard time linking the drawing, which he enjoyed, with the book, which he understood in a very limited way.

This glimpse of students' perceptions captures many of our dilemmas in assessing student performance. How do we find out what they really understand? How do we encourage them to integrate their experiences and develop new understandings?

This chapter presents a Mindful Learning approach to assessment. The first section explores assessment as an issue and offers insights from studies in the middle grades. These studies suggest four principles of assessment practice. The rest of the chapter illustrates these four principles of Mindful assessment with examples of student work we have gathered over the past few years.

Principles of Mindful Assessment

As Herman (1992) has noted, "educational assessment is in a process of invention. Old models are being seriously questioned; new models are in development" (p. 74). One of our first "aha moments" with Mindful Learning was the recognition that we cannot teach in different ways and then use the same old tests. Much of our work in classrooms has focused on connecting students' learning in their own ways with ongoing analysis of what and how they are learning.

Evaluating students' progress in this fashion is often more difficult than it may seem. While it makes sense to assess writing by asking students to write or to assess mastery of science concepts through projects, assessing understanding based on performance is often challenging. A growing number of investigations have demonstrated how "face validity," that is a judgment based on the performance of a task itself, may not be consistent over time or reliable as a benchmark (Linn, Baker, & Dunbar, 1991; Herman, Gearhart, & Baker, 1993) To tap students' talents, teachers need performance indicators they can use with confidence.

Fortunately, studies of assessment processes are providing clear direction for developing more sophisticated measures. Zemelman, Daniels, and Hyde (1993) have reviewed large-scale studies of achievement and integrated their findings with classroom studies to identify a set of "best practices." Their analysis suggests that best practice in evaluation across subject fields means:

- The purpose of most assessment is formative, not summative.
- Most evaluation is descriptive, not scored and numerical.
- Students are involved in record-keeping and in judging their own work.
- Teachers triangulate their assessments, looking at each child from several angles by drawing on observation, conversation, artifacts, performances, etc.

- Evaluation activities are part of instruction (such as in teacher-student conferences), rather than separate from it.
- Teachers spend a moderate amount of their time on evaluation assessment, not allowing it rule their professional lives or consume their instruction.
- Where possible, competitive grading systems are abolished or deemphasized.
- Parent education programs help community members to understand the value of new approaches—why, for example, a portfolio of work samples actually provides far better information about student growth than an "83" or a "B–." (p. 189)

Based on their conclusions regarding best practice in evaluation, we have generated a set of principles for Mindful assessment:

1. Assessment should involve students.
Mindful Learning begins with students' understanding of how they learn. Learning to assess their own understandings and to monitor their own progress is essential to academic success and self-discipline. To make these connections, students need to understand learning goals and share responsibility for recording and assessing progress toward those goals.

2. Forms of assessment should reflect purposes.
Assessment serves two general purposes: evaluating students' understanding of content and monitoring their proficiency with learning strategies. While these two purposes are often connected, priorities for assessment should be clear. Assessment toward understanding content should focus on essential concepts: how well students demonstrate mathematical problem solving or how well they describe literary characters, for example. Assessment toward proficiency should focus on learning strategies such as reading comprehension or writing for different audiences.

3. Assessment should be ongoing.
As indicated in earlier chapters, learning is most Mindful when students can connect what they are learning with how they learn. While every instructional activity is an opportunity for teachers to assess understanding and progress, benchmark performances should be assessed periodically in a systematic fashion.

4. Assessment decisions should reflect as many data sources as possible.
Summative judgments such as grades or scores should represent a series of performances, not just a single test. Teachers can record observations, review assignments, and confer with students.

Developing Assessments for Mindful Learning

As indicated above, assessment serves two general purposes: evaluating students' understanding of content and monitoring their proficiency with learning strategies. On a day-to-day basis, these purposes are closely intertwined. Experiences in understanding content provide opportunities to develop proficiency and vice-versa. When developing assessments, it is often helpful to identify primary purposes and structure evaluations to focus on either content or strategies. Once these procedures are structured and students understand purposes, varied forms of assessments can be used side-by-side or integrated in creative ways.

Teaching with strategies in a diagnostic fashion

Diagnostic teaching is the most powerful way to connect instruction and assessment. Often, when students experience difficulty, teachers try to "reteach" them using the same strategies. Diagnostic teaching approaches remediation differently. Instead of reteaching, diagnostic teaching "recycles" instruction, offering students a systematic opportunity to re-experience instruction with a more precise focus on ways of knowing. In other words, diagnostic teaching teaches to students' strengths. At the same time, diagnostic teaching provides the teacher with a wealth of information about what a particular student knows and what he or she finds confusing. Perhaps more importantly, the teacher can develop an ongoing profile of ways a particular student learns best—what types of activities promote understanding, what types of questions encourage connections, what types of questions yield insights. Figure 5.1 lists the basic procedures for diagnostic teaching as they relate to the planning guide for Mindful Learning.

Figure 5.1 - Diagnostic Teaching

Planning Guide for Teaching Mindful Mindful Learning Lessons	Planning Guide for Teaching Learning "Diagnostic" Lessons
GENERAL PROMPT: Tell me about this task (assignment, story, problem, etc.)	

1. What matters most about this topic?

2. What type of connections can we create between their needs and interests and this new content?

3. How can we encourage students to understand their personal ways of learning?

4. What type of varied activities can we develop to engage students in "hands on/minds on" learning? (How can we incorporate all seven frames of mind: linguistic, logical-mathematical, spatial, musical, bodily-kinesthetic, interpersonal intrapersonal?)

5. How can we relate this topic to real-world situations and encourage problem solving?

6. How will we assess learning?
   a. What will students do to demonstrate their knowledge?
   b.. How can we evaluate their progress in learning concepts?

7. What types of concluding activities will help students integrate ideas and create new connections?

8. How can we enhance teamwork?

---

1. Ask how solving problems like this one helps students at school? outside of school?

2. Ask the student to tell about other similar problems.

3. Ask the student if it would help to draw a picture? use objects? act it out? think it through step-by-step? work alone?

   PROMPT: Please show me how you think it through (if successful, go to step #6; if student has difficulty, go to step #4).

4. Using the student's responses to #3, present a guided mini-lesson. For example, reread the problem and draw a diagram or use manipulatives with the student.

5. Present a similar task and ask the student to perform that task using a similar procedure.

6. Record observations and responses.
   a. What does the student do well?
   b. What steps seem difficult?
   c. what types of prompts and suggestions seemed to be helpful?

7. Ask the student to think back over the lesson and describe the connections made.

   **Repeat steps 4–7 using similar frames of mind.

8. Meet with teammates, parents and/or administrators to develop support strategies.

The procedures outlined in Figure 5.1 provide a systematic approach to describing students' ways of knowing and linking their approaches to learning to the mastery of specific concepts. A typical scenario for diagnostic teaching might go as follows:

Teacher: Let's take a look at this quiz we took yesterday (shows Mandy the math problem she had worked the day before. Tell me how you worked this out.

Problem: Jack gave a party for 4 of his friends. He spent $2.00 on chips, $2.50 on soft drinks, and $6.00 on pizza. About how much did he spend feeding each person?)

Mandy: Well, I wasn't really sure how to do this.

Teacher: What was the first thing you thought when you saw this?

Mandy: It's similar to the problem we had last week only the stuff is different. The last one was about cookies—we figured out how much the ingredients cost.

Teacher: That's a good place to start. How do problems like these help us outside of school?

Mandy: I guess if I get to plan out a party or something—I might need to know how much it will cost.

Teacher: Would it help to start with a few things to move—like we did with the ingredients for the cookies?

Mandy: Maybe so.

Teacher: Let's say this empty cracker wrapper is the chips, the soda can is the soft drinks, and this little box represents the pizza.

Mandy: That's not a very good looking pizza.

Teacher: (laughs) Well, these are "symbolic" objects. Now, look at the problem, how can we use this stuff to get started.

Mandy: (reads over the problem, picks up the wrapper and the can) Well, chips cost two bucks and the drinks $2.50. I'd add them together then add in the pizza.

Teacher: Go ahead and write that down.

Mandy: (adds $2.00 + 2.50 + 6.00 = 11.50) Eleven-fifty—is that right?

Teacher: Does that sound right? (Mandy shakes her head.) Check your numbers.

Mandy: Oops, it should be ten-fifty. Now what?

Teacher: What does the problem ask you to do?

Mandy: Figure out how much per person.

Teacher: What does that mean in math talk?

Mandy: Divide? I should divide by four.

Teacher: Why four?

Mandy: Four friends

Teacher: Is Jack going to eat, too?

Mandy: I would if it were my party. I'll divide by five.

Teacher: What did you get?

Mandy: Two dollars and ten cents.

Teacher: Good job! Look back at your answer yesterday. What did you
do?

Mandy: I just added the numbers and forgot to divide. I added wrong,
too.

Teacher: Do you think you have it now?

Mandy: I think so

Teacher: I think so, too. Let's look at this next one. What approach will
help you with this one?

In this illustration, Mandy revisits the math problem from the day
before in a new way. The teacher guides her in connecting what she
knows from previous lessons with this problem. The teacher gives
her options along the way and draws upon the "artifacts" approach
they had used earlier. As this lesson unfolds, Mandy learns more
about solving math problems and about her own ways of learning.

This type of diagnostic teaching, with the focus on one-to-one connections, provides the richest source of assessment for teachers. Diagnostic teaching readily incorporates all of the principles of Mindful assessment: assessment is inseparably linked with instruction, assessment involves students immediately; it reflects clear purposes, and is ongoing; assessment decisions reflect multiple data sources.

An illustration of diagnostic teaching over time

The following excerpts from a teacher's instructional journal illustrate some of the ways that diagnostic teaching occurs over a series of sessions. In these journal entries, Jane Rawlings Eubank, a graduate student at UNC Greensboro, recorded her observations of her diagnostic teaching with Julia, a seventh grade student who requested individualized instruction in reading.

Lesson #1

The first piece of literature we read was a play called "In The Fog," by Milton Geiger. Julia loves to read plays. Before I proceeded with the lesson, I asked her what she thought would help her understand "In the Fog" better. She thought that we could write down the names of the four character's and then hold up the name card when it was that characters turn to talk. I asked her if drawing pictures would help and she got excited about doing illustrations.

I felt that pictorial displays would help Julia keep track of what characters were doing. It worked very well. Julia read the part of Dr. Benjamin Harris, a doctor from the city, and Eben, a stranger. She drew those two pictures. I played the parts of Zeke, another stranger, and the narrator. She also drew a picture of Zeke. We agreed that we did not need a picture of me as the narrator.

As we read the story, the pictures seemed to help Julia. She constantly looked at them before she or I read our characters' lines. Designing the pictures also encouraged her to ask questions about what the characters would be like before we read the actual play. For example, she thought Eben would be tall and the doctor would be short. We modified our pictures a bit as we went along, making Dr. Harris a bit heavier and Eben taller.

Julia kept up with the story rather well. I asker her the following questions:

- What in the play tells us that Zeke and Eben are strangers?
- Why do you think Zeke was not surprised by Dr. Harris's story?
- What would you have done in this situation if you had been Dr. Harris?
- What does "In the Fog" mean? Is it a good title for this selection?
- What atmosphere (had to define this as feeling for Julia) does the author create in the opening scene of the play? Read me the lines that create this "scary feeling."

While she answered the first four questions easily, Julia had difficulty finding the lines that the author used to create the "scary feeling." She also showed a tendency to skip lines or reread lines she had just read. I found that it helped her to use a pencil to keep track of our place as we read.

Lesson #2

The second piece of literature we read together was a short story, "Lose Now, Pay Later" by Carol Farley. I decided that this time, I would use the approach of generating questions about the text as well as give Julia a comprehensive quiz at the end of reading and discussing the story.

I decided to select some questions that would help Julia think critically about the text. Although the questions were not self-generating, I wanted her to ask herself these questions when she read the story on her own. Listed below are the questions I asked and the answers she generated. I have noted the responses that I offered when she had difficulty (marked by "teacher" in parentheses).

Questions:

1) What is a yen? (Did not know)
2) Is the woman trustworthy?
   - Yes—She is skinny, so she must use the machine. (Julia)
3) What purpose does Trevor serve in the story?
   - provides an objective view of swoodies and slimmers (teacher)
   - offers a contrast to all of the characters (teacher)
4) Are Deb and Trinja right to reject Trevor's story?
   - Yes-Everyone, including the Health Brigade Corp, seems to think that swoodies and slimmers are great (Julia)
5) At the end of the story, Deb says, "Humans would never sacrifice their freedom and dignity just so they could eat and still be thin." Do you agree or disagree?
   - No—In real life, many people are *addicted* to things that offer instant gratification but are not good for them (alcohol, cigarettes, certain foods, drugs). (Julia)
6) Which characters in this story have tunnel vision?
   - Deb, Trinja and other swoodie lovers have tunnel vision— they spend their days waiting to eat swoodies and going to slimmers and lose their ability to think critically.(Julia)
7) What were your thoughts as you finished reading the story?
   - "It was good."
   - "It could not happen." (Julia)

My intent for these discussion questions was to have Julia draw inferences from the story by actively monitoring her comprehension. I am trying to show her that good readers slow down when they are confused and check their understanding. Julia sometimes reads on and does not employ self-questioning strategies. I feel that our discussion helped her comprehend what was happening in the story.

Lesson #3

As I prepared for our next session, I felt that it would be best to employ a content analysis. The purpose of a content analysis is to help students and teachers identify facts, concepts, and generalizations presented in a given unit of study. By carefully analyzing a new unit of study, the student and teacher can locate important information and disregard trivia. Hence, the development and use of visual displays, such as graphic organizers, can portray the organization and depict the relationships among pieces of information.

As indicated in Chapter Four, a graphic organizer is basically a chart that is distributed to students prior to beginning a new unit of study. The chart presents the essential information to be understood (**see page** 000). It provides a means for presenting new vocabulary in the unit, showing relationships of vocabulary to larger concepts and generalizations, and helping students and teachers clarify teaching goals.

After we read an entry about folklore in a textbook, we identified all the facts and vocabulary we felt was essential to understanding. This forms the bottom layer of information, or subordinate concepts. The list looked like this:

- Folklore
- Myths
- Folk Tales
- Fables
- Legends
- Creation Myths
- Trickster Tales

After listing this information, we grouped related facts into clusters. These clusters form a second layer of understanding in the unit, which is referred to concepts. Finally, we related concepts to form a graphic organizer (see page 152).

Once I provided the first example, Julia picked up the activity right away. It seemed that the organizer helped her bridge the gap between ideas and language structures.

Lesson #4

The next lesson focused on creating a summary. I explained that the next piece we were going to read was titled "The Magic Season," by Susannah Harris Stone and Mir Tamim Ansary, and asked her if she could guess what we would be reading about? Once I prompted her with the fact that the story had something she liked to

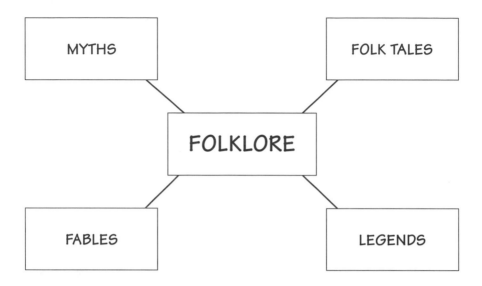

participate in, she guessed it was about Earvin Johnson, better know as Magic.

After we read the story" The Magic Season," I asked Julia to write down a summary of the story as she typically would. The following is what she wrote, without assistance (after spell-check):

> In the first year of real basketball, Magic was asked to lead his team into the playoffs. Kareem Abdul-Jabbar also was on his team because he plays too. He was called Magic because of his ball handling. The Lakers finish first in the championships. Kareem Abdul-Jabbar watched.

After Julia wrote her summary of the story, we discussed the main idea, that Magic was a young, promising basketball player. Then we rewrote the summary to provide a more thorough report. Finally, we developed a topic sentence. The following paragraph is what Julia wrote after our discussion:

> In the first year of real basketball, Magic was asked to lead his team into the playoffs. Magic had worked hard as a kid at the game of basketball and had

played well in high school and college in 1979. The Los Angeles Lakers were getting ready for their first game of the season and Magic was starting his first day of professional basketball. Kareem Abdul-Jabbar was also on his team. The Lakers were playing San Diego and they won. Magic was happy and hugged Kareem. But in game 5 Kareem hurt his ankle so Magic played center for him. He scored 42 points. Magic went on to be a great basketball player.

Recommendations

Based on our work to date, I have six suggestions for Julia to continue improving her reading skills. First, Julia seems to need an interactive environment. I have found that lively conversation helps engage Julia in learning. Her teachers and/or parents may take turns leading discussions about topics in the text. This "interpersonal" emphasis really helps Julia.

Second, we should encourage Julia to read and re-read text to develop word recognition. Repeated reading of text appears to help Julia identify terms and comprehend better. She is able to generalize the skills and words learned to other texts. One approach to doing this is to provide a situation in which Julia reads the text silently while listening to someone else read the text orally. By hearing the text, Julia is receiving correct feedback on word pronunciation

Third, Julia would benefit from more practice with computers. There are several advantages to using a computer to provide practice and reinforcement. Julia seems interested in learning more about reading-related software.

Fourth, Julia needs to begin to use metacognitive strategies to remember and to monitor understanding of word meanings. Although Julia may have a firm grasp of the meaning of a familiar object such as "couch," the ability to accurately understand and recall the meaning of an unfamiliar technical term is limited.

Fifth, self-monitoring skills are important for Julia to independently regulate her own comprehension and remember what words mean. A critical goal of instruction in the area of vocabulary is for her to become a more autonomous learner, monitoring her own understanding of the words she is reading.

Finally, Julia needs to practice reading critically and drawing inferences. Similar cognitive processes underlie critical thinking and reading comprehension. Reading and critical thinking reflect high level intellectual processes, for they require interrelationships of a number of factors.

I feel that Julia has made progress and that we have accomplished several basic aspects during our reading sessions. For instance, during the first two reading sessions, Julia would read the material without thinking about it in a critical manner. Now, she tries to get an overall sense of the reading. We still need to improve the use of other strategies such as drawing on her knowledge from other reading or her own experience.

I also feel that Julia's reading has become more active. She is beginning to use the immediate text to shape her reading by flipping back to earlier pages.

Julia has the tools to improve her reading which will strengthen other content areas in turn. While she is not a risk-taker in reading, she is receptive to learning and acquiring knowledge. When she gains more confidence in her ability to read fluently, I believe that she will begin to try more difficult books and absorb as much knowledge as she possibly can.

Understanding content

Jane Eubanks record of her work with Julia demonstrates some of the ways that diagnostic teaching can provide a powerful link between assessment and instruction. This form of assessment works best when teachers can work with students one-on-one. In the daily flow of lessons, other forms of assessment become essential, especially when teachers need to conduct assessments with large numbers of students.

When the primary focus of assessment is the extent to which students understand content area concepts, teachers can evaluate performance in a step-by-step fashion. Basic procedures are

STEP ONE—Define the concepts students will learn.

STEP TWO—State general expectations and describe the ways students will demonstrate their learning.

STEP THREE—Develop rubrics for each project option. (A rubric is a scoring guide that defines expectations for each level of performance and connects key concepts with performance options.)

STEP FOUR—"Test" rubrics with samples of student work and revise them to "fit."

STEP FIVE—Ask students to evaluate their own learning.

Illustration: To show how these steps can structure assessment, the illustrations that follow demonstrate some of the ways Ms. Johnson might assess her students' learning during the unit on "Adolescence" described in Chapter One (see pages 7–12).

STEP ONE: Define the concepts students will learn.
Beginning with the passage "Adolescence" from the *Integrated Science* text (**see page 000**), Ms Johnson might identify the following *key concepts*:

- physical growth is often uneven during adolescence and affects people in different ways
- uneven growth may result in concerns regarding one's appearance
- the onset of puberty results in emotional turbulence as well as physical changes
- adolescence is often a time of identity formation and value development

STEP TWO: State general expectations and describe the ways students will demonstrate their learning.
Having identified key concepts to guide instruction, Ms. Johnson might next decide that students should demonstrate one or more of the basic concepts of the unit. "Grades " would reflect the extent to which they can express concepts clearly and thoroughly.
As described on page 10, she collaborated with her students to generate five project options for her unit:

1. Create a portrayal of one or more developmental changes of adolescence. These could be drawings, paintings, collages, or sculptures.
2. Select a song that captures adolescent feelings and present a critique (in writing or in speech).
3. Design and administer a survey about developmental transitions. Compile and analyze results.
4. Analyze a short story or news report that deals with adolescence.
5. Write your own autobiography from birth through age thirty. Include a timeline showing developmental changes and other changes that occur over time.

STEP THREE: Develop rubrics for each project option.
For each of the five project options, Ms. Johnson and her students might develop rubrics like those that follow for Option 1 "Create a portrayal," and Option 3, "Design and administer a survey."

Option 1. Create a portrayal of one or more developmental changes of adolescence. These could be drawings, paintings, collages, or sculptures.

RUBRIC: Students who submit artwork will be asked to explain to the teacher what they hope to represent. Teachers will ask a "panel of judges" (other teachers) to study the work and judge the degree to which students communicated their ideas clearly and creatively.

GUIDELINES:

Minimum "C"—Judges agree that the project portrays one aspect of the concept identified.

"B"—Judges agree that the project is accompanied by a written or verbal statement that clearly defines the relationship of the art product to the concept.

"A"—Judges agree that the project is accompanied by a written or verbal statement that clearly explains two or more aspects of the relationship of the art product to the concept.

Option 3. Design and administer a survey about developmental transitions. Compile and analyze results.

GENERAL EXPECTATIONS:

1. Survey questions address all three concepts.
2. The survey includes:
   - 10 questions minimum
   - Report of results
   - Analysis of results
   - Conclusion
3. Survey must be administered to three different populations that vary by age, gender, and/or ethnic background.

GUIDELINES:

1. The survey design should clearly address one or more of basic concepts.
   - 5 points per concept
   - Section total: 20 points.
2. Accurate mathematical computations.
   - 2 points off per error
   - Section total: 20 points
3. Survey must be administered to three different populations according to age, gender, and/or ethnic background.
   - 10 points per group

- Section total: 30 points
4. Analysis must show relationships(s) between physical development and emotional impact.
   - 10 points per group
   - Section total: 30 points

Grading scale:

90–100 = A

80–89 = B

Less than 79: Project must be revised.

STEP FOUR: "Test" rubrics with samples of student work and revise them to "fit."

When Ms. Johnson tries out the rubric for Option I "Create a portrayal" that she developed with students, she might find that the judges were not clear what would constitute an acceptable written or verbal or statement. Ms. Johnson might discuss this with students and add a statement like the following to the rubric: "Statements consist of at least one paragraph or a two-minute talk."

STEP FIVE: Ask students to evaluate their own learning.

Ms. Johnson might develop questions like these to guide students in evaluating their own learning on this project:

1. List the most important new information you discovered.
2. Describe the strategies you used to gather information AND decide how well these strategies worked for you.
3. Describe any difficulties you encountered while working on this project.
4. Describe what you might do differently next time.
5. Decide what you would highlight as your best work and explain why. (adapted from Ms. Rebecca Stevens, Jackson Middle School)

In these illustrations, Ms. Johnson demonstrates the four principles of Mindful Assessment. She involved her students in the process by asking them to help design project options, rubrics, and revisions of rubrics. When they finished their projects, she asked them to evaluate their own learning. The form of this assessment reflected purpose. Since the primary focus was the content of the unit, Ms. Johnson specified concepts to be learned and used these as the basis for structuring projects and rubrics. Assessment was ongoing in that students had the rubrics in hand to use as guides as they worked on their projects. In reaching her summative judgments on the unit, Ms. Johnson could use the evaluations from the rubrics and the students self-evaluations.

Developing proficiency with learning strategies

One of the most productive means for assessing students' development of proficiency in reading, writing, computing, and studying is to create a portfolio system. Portfolios can take many forms. As defined by Griffin (1995), "a portfolio is basically a container of evidence with the contents varying depending on its purpose" (p. 1). She notes that contents can vary from "working portfolios" which contain many samples of a student's work to "showcase portfolios" containing selections of the student's best work (p. 1).

Teachers and students have many options as to what types of work to include in a portfolio. Work samples might include tests, book reports, projects, compositions, videotapes of performances, photographs, or computer files. Whatever work samples teachers and students select, portfolios are most meaningful when they include students' reflections on their work. These reflections might be structured in the form of statements written periodically or "captions" that explain and assess individual works (Griffin, 1995, p. 1).

Goerss (1993) notes that portfolios can prove very beneficial to both students and teachers. One benefit is the collaboration required among students and teachers. Another is the natural encouragement of self- evaluation and the possibility for greater intrinsic motivation as students set new goals for themselves. Studies have indicated that students develop more responsibility (Lynn, 1994), learn to clarify and evaluate their own thinking, (Sanborn and Sanborn, 1994), and give teachers and parents concrete data with which to monitor progress (Collins and Dana, 1993).

Portfolios should be structured according to purpose. Columba and Dolgos (1995) describe three basic forms:

1. Showcase portfolios—students' best work
2. Teacher-student portfolio—working portfolios that provide a basis for conferencing about works and progress

3. Teacher Alternative Assessment portfolio—work that is evaluated (graded or scored)

With all three types of portfolios, conferencing becomes an essential process. If students are to benefit from portfolios, they need to discuss their works with teachers, peers, and parents. When these conferences are structured for students to show what they can do correctly, conferences become a dynamic process for enhancing self-esteem (Columba and Dolgos, 1995).

Illustration: The guidelines that follow present a structure for developing portfolios of reading strategy assignments.

Guidelines for Reading Portfolios

Goals: Students will improve reading comprehension through the use of three strategies:

a) highlighting (for understanding information that is "right there")
b) charting (for "think & search" comprehension)
c) using "mindful learning" for personal applications (or "on your own" comprehension)

Directions:
1. Complete sample lesson which introduces procedures for reporting reading activities.
2. Select reading passages to include with your portfolio. Passages which you read and discuss with a teacher or classmate will be placed in the Guided Reading Folder. For each entry, please place a copy of the passage in the folder and complete the logbook as follows:

date	title of passage	read by myself (check mark)	read with teacher (check mark)	read with_____ (list name)

3. Passages which you select for reporting will be placed in the Reading Reports Folder. These should be passages you choose to spend some time with and use as the basis for a project. Place a copy of the passage in the folder and complete the logbook as follows:

date	title of passage	type of notes created (list)	type of organizer created (list)	type of project (list name)	reflections completed (checkmark)

4. See sample lesson for your options charts, projects, and reflections.

Sample Lesson:
1. Read the passage "Technology Close-Up." As you do so, take notes on the passage.

OPTIONS FOR TAKING NOTES INCLUDE:

A. HIGHLIGHTING—Use your highlighter pen or a pencil to underline important ideas and circle key words.
B. MARGIN NOTES—Write key words or big ideas in the margin.
C. VOCABULARY CARDS—Write important words on cards to use to study.
2. Create an organizer for information from the passage. The organizer should fit the type of text passage you have read. General options for organizing information include:
A. Concept Guides—Passages like this one emphasize lists of ideas. For this type of passage, you can make a "listing" chart like the one that follows. Steps include
1. Review your notes on the passage (highlights, margin notes, or cards).
2. List several key terms on a sheet of paper and see how they relate to each other. From the first two paragraphs, your notes might include "spinoff," "bicycle helmets," and "athletic shoes."

Figure 5.2

Technology Close-Up ━━━━

The space program has affected all of our lives in ways which are not always obvious. There are many new products which are "spinoffs" of the technology developed to allow man to travel in space. A spinoff has been transferred to a use different from its original purpose.

Perhaps you like to play sports. You may not believe how much space technology has contributed to developing athletic products. Bicycle helmets, boomerangs, and sailboard fins have all used space technology to improve their designs. Even athletic shoes have adapted material from space-suits to be better cushioned.

Space technology has had a lot of applications in medicine. Laser heart surgery, blood pressure control, aids for the handicapped, and dialysis equipment are all using NASA technology. Doctors can use computer image enhancement technology that was developed to read satellite photographs as a way to see into the human body. The nickel-cadmium battery used in space probes has also improved pacemakers. Even a special chair that reduces stress has a design based on the seats in the Space Shuttle.

Space technology has many safety applications, including flame-retardant clothing, water treatment systems, and lightning protection. One safety application of NASA technology that affects you every day is the improvement of safety and reliability of school buses.

There are thousands of other ways in which technology affects what you do every day. Can you think of some? Spinoff technology is one way the space program has improved life on earth as well as advanced the exploration of space.

This NASA satellite image can benefit agriculture.

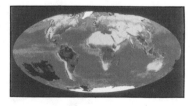

Source: Hill, S.R. Shaw, R. Stiffler, L.E. and Lacy, L. (1994) *Integrated Science: Systems and Diversity.* Durham, North Carolina: Carolina Academic Press.

3. Identify a big idea to serve as organizer. The big idea should describe relationships among the important words. In this case, products in stores (like boomerangs) are "spinoffs" from NASA.

4. Arrange a chart that shows the relationship you have found. For example:

Original NASA Invention	Spinoff
batteries used in space probes	batteries used in heart pacemakers

B. Flow Charts—Flow charts include timelines and "decision trees" that show relationships with arrows. Flow charts are most useful when the information follows an "if, then" sequence or tells about events in order. For an example of a flow chart, see page 000 (DECIDE strategy)

C. Graphic Organizers—Graphic organizers are diagrams that show relationships between words in a passage. Steps include

1. Identifing important words and ideas from the text passage.

2. Arranging terms on a sheet of paper in a way that reflects the relationships among them.

3. Adding artwork to provide a visual reference for each of the terms. Page 164 offers an example for the passage "Technology."

D. Log Books—Log books are useful in organizing events that tell us about a character. They are often written in a "diary form" or as entries in a calendar. A sample format might be

Monday—Today I...

Tuesday—The most unusual thing happened today

Wednesday—Let me tell you about...

3. Create a project to express your ideas from the passage and demonstrate your understanding. Explain to the teacher what you hope to represent. Teachers will ask a "panel of judges"

"TECHNOLOGY"
NASA spinoffs

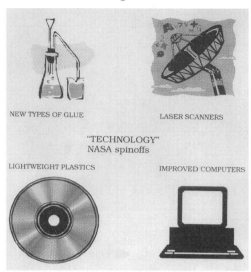

NEW TYPES OF GLUE   LASER SCANNERS

"TECHNOLOGY"
NASA spinoffs

LIGHTWEIGHT PLASTICS   IMPROVED COMPUTERS

(other students and teachers) to study the work and judge the degree to which you have communicated your ideas clearly and creatively. Project options might include:

A. Art—Create an expression of one or more of your ideas. These could be drawings, paintings, collages, or sculptures. Another option is to combine your ideas in a poster that offers many words and pictures.

B. Music—Select a song that expresses ideas from the passage and present a reaction (in writing or in speech). Another option is to select portions of songs on CD's that express ideas and tape these "sound bites" onto an audiotape.

C. Using objects—Decorate the outside of a paper bag with pictures that express ideas from the passage. Put objects that represent ideas in the bag.

D. Drama—Act out ideas from the passage or work with other students in performing a skit or role playing presentation.

E. Technology—Use a multimedia package (like HyperStudio) to create your presentation of your ideas.

F. Interviews—Prepare a set of interview questions about the ideas in the passage and ask at least five people to answer the questions. Report what they said and how their ideas related to yours.

G.Other ideas—Share your own ideas for projects with the teacher.

4. Please evaluate your own learning of this passage as follows:

A.Describe the strategies you used to gather information and decide how well these strategies worked for you.

B. Describe any difficulties you encountered while working on this project and what you might do differently next time.

C.Decide what you would highlight as your best work and explain why.

Illustration: To show how these directions can be applied to individual work, I asked our son Alex (age 10) to create a portfolio to include in this text. His contributions are as follows:

NAME: Alex Strahan

date	title of passage	read by myself (check mark)	read with teacher (check mark)	read with_____ (list name)
9/12	QUEST FOR THE GOLD CH. 1 DREAM TEAMS	✓		
9/13	QUEST FOR THE GOLD CH.11, ANFERNEE HARDAWAY	✓		
9/14	NBA BOOK OF FANTASTIC FACTS, PAGES 11–15	✓		
9/15	NBA BOOK OF FANTASTIC FACTS, PAGES 15–20		✓	
9/14	NBA BOOK OF FANTASTIC FACTS, PAGES 55–57		✓	

date	title of passage	type of notes created (list)	type of organizer created (list)	type of project (list name)	reflections completed (checkmark)
9/14	NBA BOOK OF FANTASTIC FACTS, PAGES 11–15	LIST OF FACTS			
9/15	NBA BOOK OF FANTASTIC FACTS, PAGES 15–20	SPORTS REPORT			
9/16	NBA BOOK OF FANTASTIC FACTS, PAGES 55–57	LIST OF FACTS	TIMELINE	DRAWING & ESSAY	✓

ALEX'S NOTES

9/14 - PENNY HARDAWAY - BORN JULY 18, 1972, MEMPHIS, TENN.

 REAL NAME = ANFERNEE

 GOT HIS NICKNAME "PENNY" FROM MISTRANSLATION OF GRANDMA'S NICKNAME "PRETTY"

 WENT ON TO GLORIOUS CAREER AT MEMPHIS STATE

9/15 - DENNIS RODMAN

 DENNIS RODMAN IS NOT YOUR AVERAGE NBA STAR. HE HAS DYED HIS HAIR RED, BLUE, ORANGE, AND GREEN. ONE CHRISTMAS HE WORE RED AND GREEN COMBINED. A SPORTSCASTER ONCE SAID THAT "RODMAN HAS MORE TATOOS THAN A SHIP FULL OF SAILORS. THE TRUTH IS THAT RODMAN IS FAMOUS NOT JUST BECAUSE HE IS DIFFERENT BUT BECAUSE HE CAN PLAY. HE HAS MADE A NAME FOR HIM-

SELF AS A DEFENSIVE DEMON AND REBOUNDING MACHINE. TEAMMATES LIKE ISIAH THOMAS AND DAVID ROBINSON HAVE COMMENTED THAT HE IS AS VALUABLE FOR HIS DEFENSE AS OTHERS ARE FOR THEIR POINTS. BOTH ALSO PRAISE HIS IN-TENSITY. ROBINSON SAID "HIS SPIRIT AND HUSTLE ARE AMAZ-ING."

9/16 - MICHAEL JORDAN

| BORN FEB. 16, 1963 BROOKLYN, NY | GREW UP IN WILMINGTON, NC | MARCH 29, 1982 FRESHMAN, UNC HITS GAME WINNING JUMPER WITH 17 SECONDS LEFT "THAT SHOT PUT ME ON THE BASKETBALL MAP." | 1996 SEASON WINS 4TH NBA CHAMPIONSHIP AND MVP |

9/16 - PERSONAL ESSAY

THIS IS WHY I THINK THAT THESE THREE PLAYERS' JERSEYS WILL BE RETIRED AS "THE GREATS." LET'S START WITH DENNIS RODMAN. I LIKE DENNIS BECAUSE OF HIS HAIR AND HIS SHORT FUSE. THE REAL REASON I LIKE RODMAN IS THAT DENNIS IS THE BEST RE-BOUNDER IN HISTORY. NEXT, LET'S GO WITH PENNY HARDAWAY. I LIKE PENNY BECAUSE HE IS GOOD. HE SCORES LOTS OF POINTS AND HE CAN DUNK. I ALSO LIKE HIM BECAUSE HE SEEMS LIKE A NICE GUY AND HIS BASKETBALL CARDS ARE WORTH A LOT OF MONEY. LAST, MICHAEL JORDAN IS THE BEST BASKETBALL PLAYER EVER IN THE HISTORY OF BASKETBALL. HE HAS WON FOUR CHAM-PIONSHIPS IN A ROW IF YOU DON'T COUNT HIS YEAR OF RETIRE-

A WAVE OF THE FUTURE

RODMAN 91 JORDAN 23 HARDAWAY 1

MENT TO PLAY BASEBALL. I LIKE TO COLLECT BASKETBALL CARDS
BECAUSE THEY ARE COOL LOOKING, WORTH MONEY, AND IT IS FUN.
THESE ARE MY OPINIONS BUT YOU MIGHT BEG TO DIFFER.

Assessing progress toward self-discipline

These illustrations show that rubrics and portfolios can be productive tools for assessing progress and planning instruction. In a
very natural fashion, their use fits the four principles of Mindful
assessment. Assessing students' progress toward self-discipline is
not so straightforward. Yet we are finding that the principles of
Mindful assessment can provide a framework for integrating
teachers' efforts toward positive discipline:

1. Assessment should involve students.
2. Forms of assessment should reflect purposes.
3. Assessment should be ongoing.
4. Assessment decisions should reflect as many data sources as
   possible.

As shown in Chapter Four, learning self-discipline is a process of
developing values and connecting choices and consequences. Much
of this process is learning to understand one's own thoughts and
feelings. In assessing progress toward self-discipline, teachers must
begin by helping students express their perceptions of these
thoughts and feelings. Diagnostic teaching can provide a systematic
framework for encouraging these connections.

Teachers can meet with students in conferences to "diagnose"
their processing of information related to discipline in ways very
similar to the academic diagnostics illustrated earlier in this chapter.

Illustration—For purposes of illustration, the following scenario
demonstrates how Mandy's teacher might talk with her about a
disciplinary incident in a fashion very similar to her discussion of
a math problem.

Teacher: Let's think back over this incident with Stephanie. Tell me how
you tried to work this out.
Mandy: Well, when she accused me of stealing her CD, I wasn't really
sure what to do. I got so mad I really told her off.
Teacher: What was the first thing you thought when you said that?

Mandy: Well, this kind of stuff happens all the time. She brings something to school to show it off and the next thing you know, it's missing.

Teacher: What do you think is going on?

Mandy: She loses her stuff or someone else takes it and then blames me.

Teacher: Would it help to sit down and talk this over with her?

Mandy: Maybe so.

Teacher: Let's come up with a plan for talking this over.

Mandy: I could ask her to meet with one of the peer mediators.

Teacher: What would that help you do?

Mandy: Stop yelling at each other.

Teacher: What will you need to do to make that work?

Mandy: Talk to her again. Tell her I have calmed down. Tell her I want to help her find the CD.

Teacher: Are you comfortable with that?

Mandy: I'll try it.

In this illustration, Mandy revisits the argument she has had with Stephanie in a new way, just as she revisited the math problem in the earlier scenario. As before, the teacher guides her in connecting what she knows from previous episodes with the problem. The teacher asks her to clarify her thoughts and feelings. As this discussion unfolds, Mandy learns more about the ways she is processing this information.

This type of diagnostic teaching, with the focus on one-to-one connections, provides rich information about the ways students think through the choices they make. Once students themselves are involved in analyzing choices and consequences, teachers can gather other useful data from team discussions.

Illustration—One way to show how teachers can assess progress toward self-discipline is to revisit the case of "Stan" from Chapter Four. In that chapter, a set of "team minutes" from Stan's teachers summarized how they first discussed his case in a team meeting. The team report that follows illustrates how Stan's teachers might assess his progress toward self-discipline at later meeting.

TEAM MEETING, 9/25—first period, Ms. J., recorder

Our first topic for discussion was to review our observations of Stan's behavior since our last discussion of his situation (9/11). We began by reporting how Stan was doing in our classes.

- Mr. B. reported that Stan was beginning to turn in assignments in reading. He had finished one of the books in the Book Club kit and answered most of the questions, Mr. B. was still trying to find a book that Stan would really like.
- Ms. M. indicated that Stan was doing a little better in social studies (had turned in four more homework papers, volunteered once in class, almost passed the second quiz).
- Ms. S. said that his work in language arts was also a little better (two homework grades, a first draft on the descriptive essay).
- Mr. L. reported that was still doing well in math (83% on homework, some participation, 92% on quizzes).
- I noted that his work in science was about the same (passing on lab assignments, C's on quizzes).

We then turned to Stan's behavior:

- In social studies, Ms. M. noted that he seemed to be paying attention more often, had volunteered to bring in props for a group presentation.
- In language arts, he still refused to read aloud in a class setting. Ms. S. reported that he read to her individually when they had a conference on his Book Club project.
- Mr. L. reported that Stan was still working with Mike and Alan and that their group probability project on NFL field goals was one of the most interesting in the class.
- I noted that he also did well with them on his labs in science, and that their write-ups were pretty good.
- Mr. B. noted that he had been trying to use Stan's strengths in math and science to build success in reading. He added that the Book Club selection was on football and that Stan had mentioned his math project on probability. They had played chess twice, and Stan was beginning to talk a bit more as they played, mostly about the moves and asking for advice on protecting his pieces.

We will discuss Stan's progress again next month.

Conclusions

The four principles of Mindful assessment provide a framework for evaluating students' progress toward academic achievement and self-discipline. Assessment that involves students begins with students' understanding how they learn. Assessment strategies that reflect purposes provide ways to monitor students' understanding of content and their proficiency with learning strategies. Ongoing assessments permit teachers to use day-to-day instructional activities as opportunities to evaluate understanding and progress. Assessment decisions that reflect as many data sources as possible provide a basis for comprehensive judgments and dialogue with students.

With Mindful assessment, students are involved from the very beginning. Throughout the process, they evaluate their progress

toward understanding content, expanding their repertoire of strategies and developing self-discipline. Over time, they can begin to assume more responsibility for their own learning. When that happens, evaluation becomes a natural part of the Mindful Learning process.

CLASSROOM APPLICATIONS

"Prompts to guide conferencing"

To guide conferences, Columba and Dolgos (1995) suggest the following prompts:

"The best thing about this is..."
"It was hard for me when I had to..."
"I didn't like... because..."
"I selected this piece because..."
"This piece shows that I am able to do..."
"This work shows I need to work on..."

Columba and Dolgos (1995) note that when students have an opportunity to respond to prompts such as these, they can focus on the works they have done best. Not only will they acquire a greater sense of ownership of the process, but they will also develop clearer goals for their next works.

CLASSROOM APPLICATIONS

"Using Mindful Learning to solve math problems diagnostically"

We developed the problems and questions that follow to use with students on a one-to-one basis to assess the ways they approach word problems. By following the diagnostic procedure described above with three different types of prompts (drawing, acting, listing), we have been able to determine which types of prompts are most productive in helping students make connections.

Problem #1: Linda, Rick, Chad, and Melissa were all late for school today, but each arrived separately. Chad arrived after Melissa and before Linda. When Linda arrived, Rick was not there yet. Who got to class first?

1. Tell us about this problem.

   How do problems like this one help us with other problems in school?

   outside of school?

2. Will it help to draw a picture?   yes or no

   use objects?   yes or no

   act it out?   yes or no

   think it through step-by-step   yes or no

   discuss it as a group?   yes or no

   work alone?   yes or no

3. List the steps you would follow and show your solution.

4. Did you get an answer that makes sense? If not, what could you try differently?

5. (After we draw it)—did it help you to draw it?

Problem #2: During a football game, the Panthers gained 3 yards, lost 4 yards, lost 2 yards, and gained 7 yards in four consecutive plays. How many total yards did the team gain or lose?

(After we act it out—did it help you to act it out?)

Problem #3: Rebecca spent $5.00 for the ingredients to make 8 dozen cookies. She sold each cookie for $.10. How much did she make or lose?

(After we make a list on the board—did it help you to make a list?)

RESEARCH ABSTRACTS

(summaries of two of the data-based studies referenced in this chapter as a resource for further reference and continued reading)

Herman , J., Gearhart, M., and Baker. (1993) Assessing writing portfolios: Issues in the validity and meaning of scores. *Educational Assessment, 1* (3), 201–224.

Researchers analyzed responses to standardized writing prompts and portfolios gathered from thirty-four students in grades one, three, and four. To score individual pieces and progress demonstrated in portfolio collections, they adapted a rubric developed in previous research. This rubric features a six-point scale that incorporates four subscales: focus/organization, concrete language, elaboration, and mechanics. Results indicated that portfolios can be scored consistently with a common scale, Scores on classroom assignments were especially reliable and helped focus instruction. Results reviewed inconsistencies between judgments of individual samples and judgments across collections as a whole. Authors conclude that portfolios like those analyzed in this investigation can be most useful at the classroom level and caution readers that using portfolios to assess progress across schools and systems requires very careful development and validation.

Linn, R., Baker, E., and Dunbar, S. (1991). Complex, performance-based assessment: Expectations and validation criteria. *Educational Researcher 20* (8), 15–23.

In their comprehensive analysis of changing patterns of assessment, these researchers argue for clearer criteria for evaluation assessment. Their review of studies indicates that while performance-based assessments "appear to have the potential of enhancing validity," few of the advocates of alternative assessments "have addressed the question of criteria for evaluating these measures" (p. 16). They insist that we must attempt to get beyond the "face validity" of performance measures such as portfolios and simulations and establish measures of growth we can use with confidence. They propose eight general criteria to consider:

> Consequences—Forms should fit uses and applications.
> Fairness—All students must have opportunities to learn what is being assessed.

Transfer and generalizability—Teachers should have confidence that results are consistent across locales.

Cognitive complexity—Students should demonstrate thinking rather than rehearsal.

Content quality—Tasks employed should reflect meaningful dimensions of the discipline.

Content coverage—Tasks should reflect what has been taught

Meaningfulness—Performances should reflect activities worth completing.

Cost and efficiency—Performance assessments must be affordable and practical.

CHAPTER-TO-CHAPTER CONNECTIONS

The preceding chapters presented Mindful Learning as a systematic approach to promoting caring in action in the classroom. This chapter presents a schoolwide perspective. Three fundamental connections are the basis of this perspective:

- Students learn best in caring communities.
- Recent cultural changes have made caring communities more important than ever before.
- Successful schools create caring communities by encouraging teamwork among students, parents, and teachers.

As the final chapter in the text, this perspective provides a way to envision Mindful Learning as a cooperative effort. Studies of successful teamwork provide a framework for promoting collaboration among teachers, students, and the rest of the community.

Chapter Six

Creating Caring Communities for Learning

> I wanted to be a teacher because I have always enjoyed reading and writing and thought I could make it interesting. These first three years have been a roller coaster with the kids. We've certainly had our ups and downs. I've learned to rely on my teammates. We really pick each other up. That's why I love this job. They are the best friends I have ever had.

> Three years—it is hard to believe isn't it? The old pizazz is still there with the kids. If I could just close us off and do our thing, I would stay here. As it is, I really need to transfer. This school is coming unglued. I'll go just about anywhere just to keep teaching.

These two quotes, both from teachers recognized with district-wide teaching awards, illustrate the power of teaming. These teachers joined their colleagues with great credentials from student teaching and glowing letters of recommendation. Their students love them, parents request them, and their principals nominate them for any recognition they can. After three years, one of them feels revitalized and renewed by her teammates. The other is hoping to find another school. Their experiences underscore the importance of a sense of community among teachers as well as students.

This text has emphasized "caring in action." Each chapter has shown some of the ways successful teachers connect the caring they feel for their students with the decisions they make throughout the day. These chapters have documented strategies for helping students understand how they learn best, suggestions for incorporating these strategies into lessons and units, and ways to use these strategies to help students think through the decisions they make about their schoolwork and their behavior. These applications of Mindful Learning can bring classrooms to life. This chapter shows how Mindful Learning becomes even more productive when shared. Teachers, parents, administrators, and students can work together to create caring communities for learning.

The first chapter defined "Caring in Action" as the combination of support and structure that students need to negotiate the challenges of growing up. As Noddings (1992) suggested in her "challenge to care in schools" and Ianni (1989) found in his study of "youth charters," the needs of today's students compel us to construct new visions of schooling. Throughout this text we have seen that teachers can develop classroom communities that promote caring in action. Even so, their efforts are more productive when they join forces. When an entire team enacts a Mindful Learning approach, their attempts grow more powerful. If an entire school were to support this approach, the sense of community would be even stronger.

Improving our instruction, encouraging students to think in new ways, promoting self-discipline—all of these efforts require us to work together more creatively. Fortunately, teachers have found ways to support each other and structure their work to reach these goals. This chapter begins with a review of some of the reasons why caring communities are so important.

Establishing Mindful Learning Communities

Successful teachers understand that today's students need a sense of community. While they experience the same developmental transitions that students have always faced, the culture is changing faster than ever before. This situation makes growing up an even greater challenge.

A cultural perspective on community

In today's world, the transitions from childhood to adulthood do not happen as naturally as they once did. Traditional cultures featured elaborate rites of passage, social ceremonies that marked developmental transitions in personal and tangible ways. In many cases, children grew up to take the places of their parents. They became hunters or farmers, priests or tribal leaders, mothers or fathers to their own children. Today, children do not simply take the

Figure 6.1 Reflecting on Our Own Youth: Questions to Consider

1. What was the school year when you were in seventh grade? (ex. 1966-67)
2. Who were some of your friends in seventh grade?
3. What did you do for fun—after school and on weekends?
4. In thinking back on the "pop culture" of the times, who or what was "hot?" Whose music did you enjoy? What movies did you like to see?
5. What do you recall about your family responsibilities?
6. Who were some of your teachers?
7. What do you recall about the curriculum of seventh grade? What were some of the concepts you learned for the first time?
8. What were some of your worries in seventh grade?
9. How do you think you would have described yourself?
10. How do you think your friends would have described you? How do you think your teachers would have described you?

places of their parents, nor do they participate in predictable rites of passage. Instead, transitions are complex and prolonged. When do children become young adolescents? When do young adolescents become adults? Transitions now occur in a context of striking cultural changes.

One of the best ways to initiate a discussion of the developmental needs of "today's kids" is to compare our experiences growing up with theirs. Figure 6.1 presents a set of questions to encourage reflection.

In discussions with teachers and parents, we have identified many similarities between the experiences of seventh graders, then and now. Participants often recall feelings of uncertainty about the physical changes of puberty. We remember our friends and our fears of "being different." Some of us recall how we tried to look "grown up" on special occasions and yet would run around and chase each other like younger children. Some of us remember thinking that we just could not wait to get our driver's licenses and wondering if we would ever have a girlfriend or boyfriend. Participants often agree that "today's kids" experience many of these same feelings.

As we talk about differences, participants identify several changes that have occurred in the past few decades—the hurried pace of childhood and family life, the growing pressures on families, the increasing availability of drugs, the mixed messages from the media, and the devaluing of education. In these discussions, participants often agree that it is more difficult to grow up today. They note that fewer youth have a "safety net" of extended family and friends that many of us experienced in our youth. Violence is more widespread. Sexually transmitted diseases are life-threatening. Suicide rates continue to rise. Significant numbers of students continue to leave school, physically or psychologically. Teachers express concerns about the growing percentage of "disaffected" and "disconnected" students. Parents lament the loss of "the good old days." Everyone seems concerned about discipline and motivation.

As we continue to talk, participants begin to identify some of the positive changes that have occurred as well. Today's youth are often more aware of the world around them. They know more about social injustices and environmental issues than many of us did. They are more aware of cultural differences, understand more about gender issues, and seem to have more explicit information about their own development. Participants often note that today's youth are comfortable with computers and are more adept at using technology than some of us are as adults. Technology is providing students new ways of learning. More schools are engaged in efforts to link classrooms and communities. As we think about all of these changes, we conclude that the experiences of today's kids are very similar to ours in dealing with developmental transitions, yet are very different from ours in their interactions with their cultural surroundings.

Sometimes we adults are as confused about social changes as our students are. Frustrations regarding health, welfare, and motivation among young adolescents reflect concerns for the general well-being of our communities and ourselves. In many ways, the "good old days" are a wistful myth. The changes we see in "today's kids" reflect profound changes that are occurring in our society, changes we are only beginning to understand. In this regard, it may be helpful to try to gain more perspective on our situation, to explore the cultural context of youth today.

A Call to Care

One of the most comprehensive and insightful analyses of ways that our world has changed focuses on cultural and economic transitions. Johnston (1992) analyzes these changes from an anthropological perspective. He suggests that the key question in cultural transmission has always been "How do we learn to do things the way we do things around here? (p. 46)." For most of human history, parents and caregivers could answer that question with reasonable certainty. They could draw from community traditions to help their children learn how to be successful members of their society. In recent times, however, the rapid rate of social and cultural change has made it much more difficult for parents and caregivers to answer this question with certainty. In fact, Johnston argues, in today's society, there is little certainty at all. With less consensus regarding acceptable norms,

> "learning to be" is a matter of negotiation. Suddenly, the way we do things around here is a matter of negotiation, depending largely on a set of instrumental economic values dealing with the need to provide for economic survival and in a vastly different context than which existed even a short time ago. (p. 47)

Given this uncertainty, parents and caregivers can no longer rely on the "wisdom" of their parents or even their own experiences. Traditional assumptions such as "hard work and effort will be rewarded" and "education is the key to a successful future" are no longer automatically true (p. 47).

For young adolescents, this issue starts to crystalize around the value of schooling as preparation for the future. If their school-work makes no immediate contribution to the welfare of their family or community, students may feel that school has no present or future relevance to their lives. When this happens, the drive to excel—or even to comply with school demands—diminishes greatly (p. 53). Johnston concludes that we need to redefine our concept of schooling if we are to provide the types of care and support today's kids need to become functional adults.

> It is in school that students will learn, or not learn, how to cope with human diversity; in school, habits of productive work will be learned; and finally, schools will be where our children learn to work together for broad, mutually beneficial goals. (p. 61)

As Johnston's (1992) analysis demonstrates, "today's kids" face new challenges. Not only do they struggle with the complexities of "learning how to be" and "learning how we do things" in a culture that is changing rapidly, they must also negotiate puberty and the transition from childhood to adolescence.

This dynamic places schooling in a new context. As Noddings (1992), Ianni (1989), and others have suggested, we need to develop new visions of schooling. In today's world, schools are often the only places where students experience a sense of community. Students who have little sense of family can be revitalized by supportive teams of teachers. Students who have felt "excluded" from some avenues to success can find acceptance in caring communities. They can begin to respond to teachers who are committed to meeting the needs of all of "today's kids."

Promoting teamwork among teachers

As more educators have become aware of the new demands on schooling, studies of school improvement have focused on the dynamics of translating caring into action. A growing body of studies has documented specific ways that students benefit from conscientious efforts to create more personal connections. Arhar (1992) found that interdisciplinary teaming promoted higher levels of "school bonding" among students. Goodenow (1993) showed how teacher and peer support enhanced motivation and achievement. Hayes, Ryan, and Zseller (1994) showed how students' perceptions of caring teachers emphasized interpersonal support. These studies and others have shown that teachers can work together to make big differences for students.

At the same time, studies of change processes have underscored the challenges inherent in "learning new ways of doing things around here." The types of caring schools that Noddings and others have envisioned will require concerted efforts to create a true sense of community. Such efforts can begin with clusters of teachers within a school. One way to encourage caring is to promote stronger teamwork.

The dynamics of successful teams

In recent years, a growing number of studies have emphasized the importance of teaming in almost every workplace. From production lines to corporate boardrooms, suggestions for improving productivity have emphasized teamwork. One of the most insightful studies of the dynamics of successful teams is Larson and Lefasto's (1989) analysis of *Teamwork: What must go right/what can go wrong*. Larson and Lefasto begin their study by identifying noteworthy teams from a variety of arenas. Teams in their study included championship football teams, cardiac surgery teams, corporate development teams, executive management teams, disaster relief teams, presidential commissions, and theatrical production teams. They define a team as follows:

> A team has two or more people. It has a specific performance objective or recognizable goal to be attained; and coordination of activity among the members of the team is required for the attainment of the team goal or objective. (p. 19)

Based on interviews with members of all thirty-two teams, Larson and Lefasto operationalized a set of characteristics and tested these characteristics in an analysis of thirty-two management teams. They found that successful teams shared eight essential characteristics:

1. Clear elevating goals — Goals are personally challenging and involve a sense of urgency.
2. Results-driven structure — Roles of team members and communication among them are shaped by the results to be achieved.
3. Competent team members — Members have the professional skills necessary to perform the tasks at hand and the interpersonal skills to work well together.
4. Unified commitment — While members bring different talents to the task, they integrate their efforts.
5. Collaborative climate — Members develop trust for each other and focus interactions on accomplishing shared goals.
6. Standards of excellence — Individually and collectively, members share high expectations for performance.
7. External support and recognition — While tangible rewards matter, philosophical support from the organization is an essential characteristic.
8. Principled leadership — The leader establishes vision, focuses on change, unleashes talent, and encourages risk taking.

Larson and Lefasto found that while successful teams developed these eight attributes in varied ways, unsuccessful teams shared two consistent characteristics: lack of a clear, elevating goal and lack of unified commitment. Recurring barriers to success included confusion over priorities, tension over control issues, and self-centeredness of members.

> The most frequent complaint of members of unsuccessful teams was that the leader was unwilling or unable to deal directly and effectively with self-serving or non-contributing team members." (p. 83)

While none of the teams Larson and Lefasto studied were school-based, their findings detail the underlying personal dynamics necessary to successful teamwork.

Successful teaming in school settings.

In a study entitled "The very best teams in the very best schools as described by middle school principals," George and Stevenson (1989) found that very similar personal dynamics characterize successful middle school teams. They surveyed the principals of 154 middle schools that had been recognized for excellence by professional organizations, asking them to identify and describe the "very best" teams in their schools. Results showed that administrators emphasized both academic and affective practices. In their responses, principals cited ways that students on the "very best" teams made dramatic progress on achievement tests and were recognized accordingly (p. 9). They described the strategies teams employed to monitor progress and ways that they stressed students' progress in their conferences with parents and with each other. Responses also documented the personal interactions that constitute successful teamwork, especially within the context of the school. For example, one comment noted that team members were "close professional friends but not necessarily close personal friends (p. 13)." Principals emphasized the need to balance personal issues with team priorities. Principals stressed the student-centered nature of team deliberations and provided illustrations of teams that held frequent case discussions, met beyond team time, and worked to promote teamwork.

A major theme in all responses was the importance of team identity. Examples cited included team names, logos, mascots, shirts, buttons, pins, and colors. Another aspect of identity was the importance of recognition activities such as award celebrations, field trips, picnics, intramurals, parent meetings, and team dinners. In highlighting these results, George and Stevenson concluded:

> Distinctive threads in the fabric of this data further indicated that teachers recognized the importance and urgency of helping every child succeed in specific ways, then publicly recognizing those achievements within the teams. (p. 9)

These studies indicate that the dynamics of successful teams are personal as well as organizational. Translating caring into action means developing a clear sense of mission, recognizable identity, straightforward operational procedures, and supportive communications.

In their synthesis of studies of interdisciplinary team organization, George and Alexander (1993) have identified four essential areas of middle school teaming: organization, community building, teamed instruction, and governance (pp. 250–255). Figure 6.2 presents a summary of their findings as they relate to teaming toward Mindful Learning.

Teaming in these ways will make it more likely that all students have enriched opportunities to learn and all teachers have more support for developing more successful instruction. Even so, the quality of life in classrooms will grow still richer if entire schools can begin to promote more engaging teaching.

Schoolwide teamwork toward Mindful Learning

I have invested much of my research career studying ways that middle school students and teachers view themselves and school-

Figure 6.2 Four Phases of Teaming toward Mindful Learning

Four Phases of Interdisciplinary Team Life	Applications to Mindful Learning
Phase One: **Organization** Teachers develop shared rules and procedures for managing instruction, addressing discipline, conducting conferences, and planning activities (p. 251).	Teachers can work together to establish positive expectations, develop team-based procedures for encouraging self-discipline, and establish guidelines for conferences with students and advocates,
Phase Two: **Community Building** Teachers encourage team identity through names and logos, team events, planned units, and regular home-school communication (p. 253).	Teachers can highlight learning how to learn in "town meetings" with students and parents as well as special events such as a Mindful Learning Jamboree.
Phase Three: **Teamed Instruction** Teachers collaborate through coordination of assignments, parallel curriculum planning, and inter-disciplinary units of instruction (p. 254).	Teachers can collaborate to develop strategies for creating learning profiles and for integrating teaching respect and responsibility through Mindful Learning into lessons.
Phase Four: **Governance** Teachers participate in shared decision-making processes at both the team level and school level (p. 255).	Teachers can invite students and parents to collaborate in making decisions regarding what to teach and how to teach through the establishment of a team planning council.

(George & Alexander, 1993)

ing (Strahan, 1988; Strahan, 1989; Strahan, 1990; Strahan, 1993). These investigations have illustrated ways that students and teachers make academic decisions based on their perceptions of who they are and what they think schooling should be. As I have learned more about teacher thinking, I have begun to explore connections between instructional practices and school culture (Strahan, 1992; Strahan and Leake, 1993, Strahan, 1995; Hartman and Strahan, 1997). I am convinced that we decide what to teach, how to teach, and how to respond to our students based on cultural assumptions we share with our colleagues.

While culture can be defined in many ways, the essence of culture is understanding "the way we do things around here" (Johnston, 1992, p. 46). When we stop to think about it, the "way we do things around here" reflects our collective perspectives. How we view ourselves, how we see our students, what we prize most about our subject matter—these orientations are the "core values" of teaching (Strahan, 1990, p. 240). Developing more caring core values means changing the culture of our schools. Changing "how we do things around here," means changing who "we" are. Changing these deep-seated views of ourselves and how we function can be difficult.

Studies of school improvement

Recent studies of school reform have emphasized the importance of examining shared assumptions. Van Tassel-Baska, Hall, and Bailey (1996) analyzed the nature of changes accomplished by three middle schools recognized for their efforts with school reform. They found that each of these schools accomplished structural changes such as flexible scheduling, teacher teaming, theme-based curriculum, heterogenous grouping, cooperative learning, and inclusion (p. 108). While teachers and administrators in each of these schools seemed supportive of these changes, researchers found little evidence of changes that were directly related to student learning. They concluded

> One lesson that emerged is that changing a school's philosophy and/or mission is only one step toward systemic change. Having a coherent mission, even under the guidance of a visionary leader, does not complete the school reform process. The level of change necessary needs to trickle into each classroom. This will not happen until curriculum and instruction are reformed in the same manner that structural organization has been reformed. (p. 111)

Elmore, Peterson, and McCarthy (1996) found similar patterns of change in their case studies of reform at the elementary level. Schools in their study had also accomplished structural changes such as modifying grouping practices, reorganizing teachers into teams, and empowering teachers to make decisions regarding budget and staff development. Observations of lessons indicated few changes in teaching and learning, however. The researchers concluded that transforming teaching practice is "fundamentally a problem of enhancing individual knowledge and skill, not a problem of organizational structure" (p. 240). These two studies of change processes at the school level demonstrate the complexity of changing classroom practices. They underscore the importance of examining shared assumptions of who we are and how we teach.

Studies of instructional improvement processes indicate that even though it is difficult, we can change teaching practices. Researchers have emphasized that improving instruction requires teachers and administrators to find ways to share leadership, establish priorities, create flexible organizations, and support each other continuously. In the most successful schools, adults are committed to providing personal support for students; teachers and administrators are advocates for students; and everyone feels that they are part of a team. Case studies have demonstrated the importance of dialogue. A key process seems to be finding ways to initiate and sustain meaningful conversations about the nature of "good teaching" and how to put these beliefs into practice on a day-to-day basis. These changes take time and require intensive support. To accomplish meaningful change, studies suggest that educators must address at least six issues in instructional improvement (Strahan, 1994, pp. 8–11).

1. **Time** — First, we need to acknowledge how difficult it is to make improvements that will prove worthwhile. Meaningful changes require a long time and a great deal of support. In their analyses of "self renewing schools," Joyce, Wolf, and Calhoun (1993) found that meaningful changes often require a time frame of three to five years. Studying school culture and the nature of change can help us address the complexity of changing our teaching practices.

2. **Priorities** — Joyce, Wolf, and Calhoun (1993) also demonstrated the need for establishing clear priorities. Their rule of thumb suggests that we attempt one major innovation at a time. Thinking through which one change we may approach together and which ones we might approach as teams may help guide our discussion of priorities.

3. **Practices** — We should base priorities on specific teaching practices that promote understanding. As noted above, Elmore, Peterson, and McCarthy (1996) conclude that meaningful change must begin by providing teachers access to new knowledge and skills. They suggest that changes in teaching practice are considerably more difficult to achieve and to see as they are taking place.

   Changes in teaching practice are also, as we have commented, quite sensitive to the knowledge and skills of the people who are trying to bring them about. It should come as no surprise, then, that people within and outside schools find changing structure more interesting and engaging, more motivating and energizing than changing teaching practice. The one is highly visible and sexy; the other is more difficult and indeterminate. (p. 237–238).

4. **Data** — To improve practices in a systematic fashion, we need good information about our current accomplishments. Whenever possible, we need to use data to guide decisions. Information from published studies and local research can help us select teaching practices that are most likely to enhance student learning.

5. **Shared Beliefs** — Underlying any meaningful change is a set of shared beliefs about who we are as teachers and how students learn. To make long-term improvements, we may need to question some of the assumptions that underlie our present practices. We will want to examine the notions about "how we do things around here" that shape our decisions. This is especially important when notions about how we do things around here prevent some students from feeling connected with the school. As we explore assumptions, we are likely to find that we disagree on what to do and why. How we resolve these disagreements may determine how successful we are with the innovations we have identified.

6. **Planning Processes** — Given the complexity of changing instructional practice, Fullan (1990, p. 17) concludes that we must orchestrate four connected dimensions of growth:

a. Shared purpose — Meaningful change must begin with discussions of purpose. As schoolwide teams, teachers need to discuss questions such as:

What are our "elevating goals?"

What is our vision of who we are?

b. Norms of collegiality —Collaboration requires more than congeniality. As schoolwide teams, teachers need to decide:

How can we work together to share our wisdom and pool our talents?

c. Norms of continuous improvement —Once they have identified goals and begun to work together as schoolwide teams, teachers need to evaluate improvement:

What "indicators" will we use to assess our progress?

d. Supportive organizational structure — Even the very best "workshops" result in low rates of implementation without supportive follow-up. As schoolwide teams, teachers need to explore issues such as:

How can we change our "work place" to sustain growth?

These four planning processes provide a framework for teaming at the school level. When teachers can discuss their purposes and reach agreement as to the "ways we do things around here," they can develop support processes and organizational structures to collaborate in the day-to-day tasks of teaching. They can think beyond staff development days to put theory into practice. They can identify meaningful ways to assess students' progress and, hopefully, to bring students into conversations about teaching and learning.

Mindful Learning and staff development

Studies of school improvement have emphasized that teachers need to experience new practices, not just hear about them (Elmore, Peterson, and McCarthy ,1996). Teaching practices are not likely to change unless teachers are exposed to "what teaching actually looks like when it is done differently" and to "someone who could help them understand the difference between what they are doing and what they aspire to do" (p. 241). This means opening classrooms to observers and finding time to analyze observations through discussion.

The need to experience "what teaching actually looks like when it is done differently" may also mean that we should apply what we know about "good teaching" in order to plan "good staff development." Much of what we have learned about Mindful Learning might be helpful. If some students learn best by seeing pictures or moving to learn, some of us teachers might need different types of staff development. The more "logical" among us may benefit from hypothesis-testing approaches such as piloting projects in their own classrooms in an empirical fashion. "Personal" learners may want a series of discussions with others who have tried certain teaching practices. "Spatial" learners may incorporate videotapes of practices in action. "Linguistic" learners might read published reports and share journals. Those of us who move to learn might appreciate opportunities to "walk through" certain types of lessons before trying them with students. Studies like those of Elmore, Peterson, and McCarthy (1996) remind us that learning new practices requires more than exposure.

Learning new practices also requires us to base our progress on shared benchmarks. The recommendations from The National Middle School Association's (1995) Curriculum Task Force can provide a preliminary framework for analyzing instructional practices. Figure 6.3 summarizes their recommendations.

Figure 6.3 Recommendations from The National Middle School Association's Curriculum Task Force (1995)

Conditions which should be phased out	Conditions which should be evident
Curriculum as separate subjects and skills taught and tested in isolation	Curriculum which views all areas of knowledge and skill as important and integrates these areas throughout school experiences, developed by careful and continuing study of students, social trends and issues, and research-supported school practices
Content judged to be more important than learning processes	Student exploration of integrated themes which engage them in serious and rigorous study
Students labeled and tracked into rigid ability groups	Flexible learning groups based upon students' needs and interests
Excessive use of lecturing, rote learning, and drill	Use of active collaborative, self-directed learning; staff development promotes and supports developmentally responsive practices
Domination by textbooks and worksheets	Use of a variety of educational materials, resources, and instructional strategies
Organization of faculty into departments	Staff organized in ways that encourage ongoing collaboration
Staff development efforts that are short-term and non-productive	Long-term professional growth opportunities planned by all staff

Working together to learn new practices and analyze their implementation over time can be a valuable vehicle toward extending teamwork and community.

Conclusions

Most teachers join the profession because they want to make a difference. They hope that students will learn more about the topics they love and find productive avenues for their individual talents. Most teachers try to balance their desire to teach their sub-

jects with their commitments to help students become better people. In good situations, teachers draw energy from their students and from their teammates across the hall. In difficult situations, they draw from their inner resources as best they can and try to help those around them. How well teachers work together, in their interdisciplinary teams and as schoolwide units, may be the most critical factor in school improvement.

This chapter has reviewed studies of teamwork and educational change. These studies have suggested that the essential dynamics of interdisciplinary teams—organization, community building, team instruction, and governance—are also essential to schoolwide attempts to enhance learning. While it is difficult to improve the culture of teaching, teachers can work together to identify instructional practices that best reflect "who we are and how we do things around here." Doing so takes time, requires clear priorities, demands data, and builds upon shared beliefs. Some practices should be phased out, others nurtured as carefully as the relationships which sustain them. Through debate and deliberation, teachers can share their individual and collective views of instruction and examine the principles that shape them. Most importantly, every adult in the school can watch and listen to the responses of students. Their needs for structure and support, their attempts to make sense of the world, their craving for caring that becomes action—these are the reasons for finding more Mindful ways to teach.

CLASSROOM APPLICATIONS

"Inviting school improvement:
Planning framework"

The organizer that follows provides one structure for planning and implementing meaningful improvements in teaching.

"Inviting school improvement: Planning framework"

GOAL STATEMENT:

RATIONALE:

ACTIVITIES (PRACTICES AND PROCEDURES)	TIMELINE	PERSON(S) RESPONSIBLE	ASSESSMENT STRATEGIES

RESEARCH ABSTRACTS

(summaries of two of the data-based studies referenced in this chapter as a resource for further reference and continued reading)

Arhar, J. (1990). Interdisciplinary teaming as a school intervention to increase the social bonding of middle level students. *Research in Middle Level Education: Selected Studies 1990.* Columbus, Ohio: National Middle School Association.

Arhar analyzed responses from 5000 seventh graders to a survey of social bonding. Items on the survey assessed the degree to which students felt connected to their peers, their teachers, and their school. Half of her subjects attended middle schools with teams, the other half attended non-teamed schools. Respondents represented twenty-two schools matched according to size, socioeconomic status and the percentage of minority students. Results indicated that students who attended teamed schools were more strongly bonded to both the school and their teachers. To a lesser extent, students were more bonded to their peers. Arhar concluded that school organization can enhance the social bonding of middle level students.

Goodenow, C. (1993). Classroom belonging among early adolescent students: Relationships to motivation and achievement. *Journal of Early Adolescence, 13* (1), 21-43.

Goodenow administered a School Opinion Questionnaire to 353 sixth, seventh, and eighth graders in a suburban New England middle school and analyzed their responses in relationship to their grades and teachers' ratings of their effort. The survey asked students to rate their motivation and their perceptions of the social-emotional quality of a particular class. Students were randomly assigned subject areas so that one-fourth responded in regard to each of the four core areas (language arts, math, science, and social studies). Results showed that "expectancy of success" was the primary predictor of grades and effort. Componential analysis identified three "belonging/support factors" which contributed significantly to the variance in expectancies and value: Teacher Support, Peer Support, and Belonging/alienation. Of these three, Teacher Support was the strongest predictor of expectancy, followed by Peer Support, and Belonging (p. 33). Analysis of results by grade level indicated that eighth graders relied less on the supportiveness of teachers and peers than did sixth and seventh graders (p. 37). Goodenow concludes that young adolescents' motivation must be understood as an interactive phenomenon that occurs, "not only within individuals but as developing in part out of the continuing relations between individual students and others in their social contexts" (p. 40).

Hayes, C., Ryan, A., & Zseller, E., (1994). The middle school child's perceptions of caring teachers. *American Journal of Education, 103,* **1-19.**

Researchers surveyed 208 sixth-grade students from three ethnically diverse schools in the New York City area. They collected demographic data and asked students to complete an essay response form requesting them to "think of two teachers who were memorable for their caring and to describe all that each teacher did that showed that the teacher cared" (p. 7). Analysis of data revealed eleven categories of caring "concept groups." The most frequent response was "responded to the individual." Students viewed caring teachers as providing attention outside of school and being "interested in the student's whole life" (p. 9). The next category "helping on academic work" focused on assistance beyond lessons. The third category was "encouraged success and positive feelings" followed by "provided fun and humor," "provided good subject content," "counseled the student," "interested in all students/fair," "avoided harshness," "listened," "managed class well," and "other" (p. 10). Analysis of results by demographic data showed that, like several other studies, African-American students' top three categories emphasized interdependence and interpersonal relationships (responding to individuals, helping with academic work, and encouraging success and positive feelings) more so than did European-Americans. Researchers concluded that teachers and administrators need to be more aware of the ways students perceive their practices.

Final thoughts

I often thank my grandmother for teaching me the most important things I have learned about teaching. First, I remember her as caring very, very much about her students. We used to walk through her little town in the summers. We always met at least one or two of her former students. She was glad to see them, and they were glad to see her. She spoke with them like she spoke with other adults, and like she had always spoken with me. She often invited them over to her house to help us test her new projects. While I was probably a bit jealous of other children sharing my "special" relationship with her, I knew that she was always teaching. Another insight I attribute to her is the inescapable connection between curiousity and teaching. She was always interested in everything. She read museum guides with the same passion as great novels, took me to see everything historical on every trip we ever took, and discussed "new ideas" from her magazines with a twinkle in her eyes. She collected *National Geographics* and organized them as if they were the county archives. Occasionally, we heard her say "this will make a great lesson." Most often, she was learning because she loved it.

At a recent family reunion, we realized that of my grandmother's six granchildren, four of us became teachers. Three of us married teachers. It was probably not an accident that my father became a teacher and adminstrator, or that he and my mother have provided me a lifetime course in caring.

I hope that some portion of my grandmother's passion for teaching lives on in this book.

References

Allen, L. (1996). Action research report: Motivation and multimedia. Prepared for graduate coursework at UNC Greensboro.

American Association of University Women (AAUW). (1992). How schools shortchange girls: The AAUW report: A study of major findings on girls and education. Washington, DC: AAUW Educational Foundation.

Arhar, J. (1990). Interdisciplinary teaming as a school intervention to increase the social bonding of middle level students. *Research in Middle Level Education: Selected Studies 1990,* 1–10.

Arnold, J. (1993). A curriculum to empower young adolescents. *Midpoints, 4* (1).

Barron, A. E. (1994). Multimedia research reports. *Reference Librarian, 44,* 71–82.

Beane, J. A. (1990). *A middle school curriculum: From rhetoric to reality.* Columbus, OH: National Middle School Association.

Brophy, J. E. (1983). Classroom organization and management. *The Elementary School Journal, 83* (4), 265–285.

Brown, R. (1991a). Policy and the rationalization of schooling. In E. Hiebert (Ed.), *Literacy for a diverse society: Perspectives, practices, and policies.* New York: Teachers College Press, 217–227.

Brown, R. (1991b). *Schools of Thought.* San Francisco: Jossey-Bass.

Carnegie Council on Adolescent Development. (1989). *Turning points: Preparing American youth for the 21st century.* New York: Author.

Collins, A., and Dana, T. (1993). Some notes for middle school science teachers on alternative assessment. In T. Kuerbis and S. Rakow (Eds.), *Science and the early adolescent.* Washington, DC: National Science Teachers Association.

Columba, L., and Dolgos, K.A. (1995). Portfolio assessment in mathematics. *Reading Improvement, 77* (1), 30–32.

Colvin, G., Kameenui, E., and Sugai, G. (1993). Reconceptualizing behavior management and school-wide discipline in general education. *Education and Treatment of Children, 16* (4) 361–381.

Covington, M.V. (1984a). The self-worth theory of achievement motivation: Findings and implications. *Elementary School Journal, 85,* 5–19.

Covington, M.V. (1984b). The motivation for self-worth. In *Research on Motivation in Education*. New York: Academic Press, 77–113.

Csikszentmihalyi, M., and Larson, R. (1984). Being adolescent: Conflict and growth in the teenage years. New York: Basic Books.

Csikszentmihalyi, M., and Nakamura, J. (1989). The dynamics of intrinsic motivation: a study of adolescents. *Research on motivation in education*, volume 3, 45–71.

Csikszentmihalyi, M. (1990). Literacy and intrinsic motivation. *Daedalus, 119* (2), 115–140.

Cuban, L. (1992). What happens to reforms that last? the case of the junior high school. *American Educational Research Journal, 29* (2), 227–251.

Deal, T.E. (1990). Reframing reform. *Educational Leadership, 47* (8), 6–12.

Durrant, L., Frey, D., and Newbury, K. (1991). *DISCOVER skills for life*. San Diego, CA: Educational Assessment Publishing Company, Inc.

Elmore, R., Peterson, P., and McCarthy, S. (1996). *Restructuring in the classroom : Teaching, learning, and school organization*. San Francisco: Jossey-Bass.

Epstein, J., and MacIver, D. (1990). *Education in the middle grades: An overview of national practices and trends*. Columbus, OH: National Middle School Association.

Flynt, E., and Cooter, R. (1993). *Flynt-Cooter reading inventory for the classroom*. Scottsdale, AZ: Gorsuch Scarisbrick Publishers.

Fullan, M. (1990). Staff development, innovation, and institutional development. In B. Joyce (Ed.), *Changing school culture through staff development*. Alexandria, VA: Association for Supervision and Curriculum Development.

Gabel, D. (1995). Science. In G. Cawelti (Ed.), *Handbook of research on improving student achievement*. Arlington, VA: Educational Research Service.

Gardner, H. (1983). *Frames of mind: The theory of multiple intelligences*. New York: Basic Books.

Gardner, H. (1993). *Multiple intelligences: The theory in practice*. New York: Basic Books.

Gardner, H. (1995). Reflections on multiple intelligences: Myths and messages. *Phi Delta Kappan, 77* (4), 200–209.

Gardner, H., and Hatch, T. (1989). Multiple intelligences go to school. *Educational Researcher, 18* (8), 4–10.

Garnett, K., and Bullock, J. (1991). Developing problem-solving heuristics in the middle school: A qualitative study. *Research in Middle Level Education, 15* (1), 83–103.

George, P. (1991). Student development and middle level school organization: A prolegomenon. *Midpoints, 1* (1).

George, P., and Alexander, W. (1993). *The exemplary middle school.* New York: Harcourt Brace Jovanovich College Publishers.

George, P., and Stevenson, C. (1989). The very best teams in the very best schools as described by middle school principals. *The early adolescence magazine (TEAM), 3* (5), 6–14.

Glasser, W. (1965). *Reality therapy: A new approach to psychiatry.* New York: Harper and Row.

Glasser, W. (1974). A new look at discipline. *Learning, 3* (4), 6–11.

Glasser, W. (1986). *Control theory in the classroom.* New York: Harper and Row.

Glasser, W. (1993). *The quality school teacher.* New York: Harper Perennial.

Goerss, K. (1993,). Portfolio assessment: A work in process. *Middle School Journal, 25* (2), 20–24.

Goleman, D. (1995). *Emotional intelligence.* New York: Bantam Books.

Good, T., and Weinstein, R. (1986). Schools make a difference. *American Psychologist, 41* (10), 1090–1097.

Goodenow, C. (1993). Classroom belonging among early adolescent students: Relationships to motivation and achievement. *Journal of Early Adolescence, 13* (1), 21–43.

Gottfredson, D., Gottfredson, G., and Hybl, L. (1993). Managing adolescent behavior: A multiyear, multischool study. *American Educational Research Journal, 30* (1), 179–215.

Griffin, J. (1995). Portfolio assessment in the middle school. Greensboro, NC: North Carolina Middle School Association.

Harter, S. (1990). Causes, correlates, and the functional role of global self-worth: A life-span perspective. In R. Sternberg and J. Kolligan (Eds.), *Competence considered.* New Haven, CT: Yale University Press, 67–97.

Hartman, K., and Strahan, D. (1997). How middle-level teachers communicate an ethos of caring to student teachers: A case study. Paper presented at the annual conference of the American Educational Research Association, Chicago, IL, March.

Hawk, P. (1986). Graphic organizers: Increasing the achievement of life science students. *Middle School Research: Selected Studies 1986,* 16–23.

Hayes, C., Ryan, A., and Zseller, E. (1994). The middle school child's perceptions of caring teachers. *American Journal of Education, 103,* 1–19.

Herman, J. L. (1992). What research tells us about good assessment. *Educational Leadership, 50* (2), 74–78.

Herman, J., Gearheart, M., and Baker, E. (1992). Assessing writing portfolios: Issues in the validity and meaning of scores. *Educational Assessment, 1* (3), 201–224.

Hooper, M., and Miller, S. (1991). The motivational responses of high, average, and low achievers to simple and complex language arts assignments: Classroom implications. *Research in Middle Level Education, 15,* 105–119.

Huberman, M., and Miles, M. (1984). *Innovation up close.* New York: Plenum.

Ianni, F. (1989). Providing a structure for adolescent development. *Phi Delta Kappan,* 673–682.

Irvin, J. (1990). *Reading and the middle school student: Strategies to enhance literacy.* Boston, MA: Allyn and Bacon.

Johnston, H. J. (1992). Youth as cultural capital: Learning how to be. In J. Irvin (Ed.), *Transforming middle level education.* Boston: Allyn and Bacon, 46–62.

Joyce, B., Wolf, J., and Calhoun, E. (1993). *The self-renewing school.* Alexandria, VA: Association for Supervision and Curriculum Development.

Kramer, L. (1985). Perceptions of ability in one middle school: A study of gifted adolescent females. *Middle School Research: Selected Studies 1985,* 11–33.

Larson, C., and Lefasto, F. (1989). *Teamwork: What must go right?/ what can go wrong?* Thousand Oaks, CA: Sage Publications.

Larson, J. (1992). Anger and aggression management techniques through the Think First curriculum. *Journal of Offender Rehabilitation, 18* (1/2), 101–117.

Lee, O., and Anderson, C. (1993). Task engagement and conceptual change in middle school science classrooms. *American Educational Research Journal, 30,* (3), 585–610.

Lipsitz, J. (1984). *Successful schools for young adolescents.* New Brunswick: Transaction Books.

Lynn, R. (1994). Performance assessment: Policy promises and technical measurement standards. *Educational Researcher, 23* (9), 4–14.

Lynn, R. I., Baker, E. L., and Dunbar, S. B. (1991). Complex, performance-based assessment: Expectations and validation criteria, *Educational Researcher, 20* (8) 15–23.

McGreal, T. (1988). Evaluation for enhancing instruction: Linking teacher evaluation and staff development. In S. J. Stanley and W. J. Popham (Eds.), *Teacher evaluation: Six prescriptions for success.* Alexandria, VA: Association for Supervision and Curriculum Development.

Means, B., and Olson, K. (1994). The link between technology and authentic learning. *Educational Leadership, 51* (7), 15–18.

Medick, J. (1981). *Classroom behavior: Turning it around.* East Lansing, MI: Fanning Press.

Meece, J., Blumenfeld, P., and Hoyle, R. (1988). Students' goal orientations and cognitive engagement in classroom activities. *Journal of Educational Psychology, 80,* 514–523.

Moore, D. W., and Readence, J. E. (1984). A quantitative and qualitative review of graphic organizer research. *Journal of Educational Research, 78,* 11–17.

National Association of Secondary School Principals (1986). *An agenda for excellence at the middle level.*

National Board for Professional Teaching Standards (1993). *Early adolescence/generalist standards.* San Antonio, TX: National Board for Professional Teaching Standards.

National Middle School Association (1982). *This we believe.* Columbus, OH: Author.

National Middle School Association. (1995). *This we believe: Developmentally responsive middle level schools..* Columbus, OH: Author.

National Middle School Association. (1995). Curriculum Task Force Position Paper. Columbus, OH: National Middle School Association.

Noddings, N. (1992). *The challenge to care in schools: An alternative approach to education.* New York: Teachers College Press.

Ogbu, J. G. (1992). Understanding cultural diversity and learning. *Educational Researcher, 21* (8), 5–14.

O'Sullivan, R., Harper, D., and Strahan, D. (1992). *When people who can won't! Perspectives on a teacher empowerment project from an administrator, a middle grades specialist, and an evaluator.* Paper presented at the annual meeting of the American Educational Research Association. San Francisco, CA.

Potter, R., and Hanneman, C. (1977). Conscious comprehension: Reality reading through artifacts, *The Reading Teacher,* 644–648.

Psychological Corporation. (1993). *GOALS Assessments.* San Antonio, TX: Harcourt Brace and Company.

Purkey, W., and Novak, J. (1995). *Inviting school success: A self-concept approach to teaching, learning, and democratic practice.* Belmont, CA: Wadsworth Publishing Company.

Purkey, W., and Strahan, D. (1986). *Positive discipline: A pocketful of ideas.* Columbus, OH: National Middle School Association.

Raphael, T., and McMahon, S. (1994). Book club: An alternative framework for reading instruction. *The Reading Teacher, 48* (2), 102–116.

Ringer, M., Doerr, P., Hollenshead, J., and Wills, G. (1993). Behavior problems in the classroom: A national survey of interventions used by classroom teachers. *Psychology in the Schools, 30,* 168–175.

Rubin, R. L., and Norman, J. T. (1989). A comparison of the effect of a systematic modeling approach and the learning cycle approach on the achievement of integrated science process skills of urban middle school students. Paper presented at the annual meeting of the National Association for Research in Science Teaching, San Francisco. (ERIC Document Reproduction Service no. ED 308 838).

Rubin, R. L., and Norman, J. T. (1992). Systematic modeling vs the learning cycle: Comparative effects on integrated science process skill achievement. *Journal of Research in Science Teaching, 29,* 715–727.

Sanborn, J., and Sanborn, E. (1994). A conversation on portfolios, *Middle School Journal, 26* (1), 26–29.

Scales, P. (1992). The effects of preservice preparation on middle grades teachers' beliefs about teaching and teacher education. *Midpoints, 2* (2). Columbus, OH: National Middle School Association.

Schiro, M. (1992). Educators' perceptions of the changes in their curriculum belief systems over time. *Journal of Curriculum Studies, 7* (3), 250–286.

Sizer, T. (1992). *Horace's school: Redesigning the American high school.* New York: Houghton Mifflin Co.

Smith, R., and Strahan, D. (1991). From the school of hard knocks to schools of success: Research on teachers' perceptions of students at-risk. *Transescence: The Journal of Emerging Adolescent Education, 18* (2), 4–16.

Smith, R., and Strahan, D. (1993). The evolution of preservice teachers' orientations toward teaching. Paper presented at the annual meeting of the North Carolina Association for Research in Education.

Sowell, E. J. (1981). Effects of manipulative materials in mathematics instruction. *Journal for Research in Mathematics Education, 20,* 498–505.

Sternberg, R., and Horvath, J. (1995). A prototype view of expert teaching. *Educational Researcher, 24* (6), 9–17.

Sternberg, R., Okagaki, L., and Jackson, A. (1990). Practical intelligences for success in school. *Educational Leadership, 8* (1) 35–42.

Stevenson, C. (1992). *Teaching ten to fourteen year olds.* White Plains, NEW YORK: Longman.

Strahan, D., (1985). Frames of mind: A broader view of intellectual development in the middle grades. *Journal of North Carolina League of Middle/Junior High Schools,* 8–10.

Strahan, D. (1986). Guided thinking: A research-based approach to effective middle grades instruction. *Clearing House, 60* (4), 149–155.

Strahan, D. (1987). Teachers' thoughts about student thinking: Implications for instructional improvement in the middle grades. *American Middle School Education, 10* (1), 19–27.

Strahan, D. (1988). Life on the margins: How academically at-risk early adolescents view themselves and school. *Journal of Early Adolescence, 8* (4), 373–390.

Strahan, D. (1989). Disconnected and disruptive students: Who they are, why they behave as they do, and what we can do about it. *Middle School Journal, 21* (2), 1–5.

Strahan, D. (1990). From seminars to lessons: A middle school language arts teacher's reflections on instructional improvement. *Journal of Curriculum Studies, 22* (3), 233–251.

Strahan, D. (1992). Turning points and beyond: Coming of age in middle-level research. In J. Irvin (Ed.), *Transforming middle level education.* Boston: Allyn and Bacon, 381–399.

Strahan, D. (1993). Preservice teachers' reflections on young adolescents as students and themselves as teachers. *Current Issues in Middle Level Education, 2* (2), 37–52.

Strahan, D. (1994). Putting middle level perspectives into practice: Creating school cultures that promote caring. *Midpoints, 4* (1).

Strahan, D., and Leake, B. (1993). Research for a "new" curriculum: Extending the conversation. *Research in Middle Level Education, 16* (2), 87–94.

Strahan, D., Nadolny, D., Potter, S., and Jones, J. (1993). A study of ways young adolescents describe their decisions. Paper presented at the annual meeting of the American Educational Research Association. Atlanta, GA.

Strahan, D., and Strahan, J. (1988). *Revitalizing remediation in the middle grades: An invitational approach.* Reston, VA: National Association of Secondary School Principals.

Strahan, D., and Van Hoose, J. (1987). The development of an instrument to assess teaching practices that invite success. Paper presented at the annual conference of the American Educational Research Association, Washington, DC, April.

Strahan, D., Summey, H., and Bowles, N. (1996). Teaching to diversity through multiple intelligences: Student and teacher responses to instructional improvement. *Research in Middle Level Education Quarterly, 19* (2), 43–66.

Summey, H. (1995). A case study of two sixth grade language arts inclusive classrooms. Unpublished doctoral dissertation. University of North Carolina at Greensboro.

Summey, H., and Strahan, D. (1995). Mainstreamed seventh graders' responses to a mindful learning approach to language arts instruction: A case study. A paper presented at the annual meeting of the American Educational Research Association, San Francisco.

Summey, H., and Strahan, D. (1997). The dynamics of inclusion in sixth grade language arts: Insights from two classrooms. *Research and Special Education, 18* (1), 36–45.

Tye, B. (1987). The deep structure of schooling. *Phi Delta Kappan,* 281–284.

Uprichard, A. E., and Phillips, E. R. (1982). A process-product diagnosis of problem-solving abilities—Mathematical word problems. Paper presented at the meeting of the Research Council for Diagnostic and Prescriptive Mathematics, Amherst, NY.

Van Hoose, J. (1989). An at-risk program that works. *Middle School Journal, 21* (2), 6–8.

Van Hoose, J. (1992). A/A across the day. *Midpoints, 2* (1).

Van Hoose, J., and Strahan, D. (1988). *Young adolescent development and school practices: Promoting harmony.* Columbus, OH: National Middle School Association

Van Hoose, J., and Strahan, D. (1991). "Politically astute" processes for middle level improvement. *NASSP Bulletin, 75* (532), 63–72.

Van Hoose, J., and Strahan, D. (1992). Nurturing personally and professionally inviting behaviors through a clinical supervision model. In J. Novak (Ed.), *Advances in Invitational Thinking.* San Francisco,CA: Cado Gap Press.

Van Tassel-Baska, J., Hall, K., and Bailey, J. (1996). Case studies of promising change schools. *Research in Middle Level Education Quarterly, 19* (2), 89–116.

Vaughn, J., and Estes, T. (1986). A self-monitoring approach to reading and thinking (SMART). In *Reading and reasoning beyond the primary grades.* Boston, MA: Allyn and Bacon.

Voight, C. (1986). *Izzy, Willy Nilly.* New York: Macmillan Publishing Co.

Walberg, H. (1995). Aligned time on task. In G. Cawelti (Ed.), *Handbook of research on improving student achievement.* Arlington, VA: Educational Research Service.

Wang, M., Haertel, G., and Walberg, H. (1993). Toward a knowledge base for school learning. *Review of Educational Research, 63* (3), 249–294.

Zemelman, S., Daniels, H., & Hyde, A. (1993). *Best practice: New standards for teaching and learning in America's schools.* Portsmouth, NH: Heinemann.

Index